FLOYD CLYMER'S

The Book of the
BOND MINICAR

A PRACTICAL HANDBOOK COVERING ALL MODELS UP TO AND INCLUDING THE MARK G, WITH INFORMATION ON THE 875 AND RANGER 875

BY

R. H. WARRING

THIRD EDITION
1968

ANNOUNCEMENT

By special arrangement with the original publishers of this book, Sir Isaac Pitman & Son, Ltd., of London, England, we have secured the exclusive publishing rights for this book, as well as all others in THE MOTORCYCLIST'S LIBRARY.

Included in THE MOTORCYCLIST'S LIBRARY are complete instruction manuals covering the care and operation of respective motorcycles and engines; valuable data on speed tuning, and thrilling accounts of motorcycle race events. See listing of available titles elsewhere in this edition.

We consider it a privilege to be able to offer so many fine titles to our customers.

FLOYD CLYMER
Publisher of Books Pertaining to Automobiles and Motorcycles

2125 W. PICO ST.   LOS ANGELES 6, CALIF.

INTRODUCTION

Welcome to the world of digital publishing ~ the book you now hold in your hand, while unchanged from the original edition, was printed using the latest state of the art digital technology. The advent of print-on-demand has forever changed the publishing process, never has information been so accessible and it is our hope that this book serves your informational needs for years to come. If this is your first exposure to digital publishing, we hope that you are pleased with the results. Many more titles of interest to the classic automobile and motorcycle enthusiast, collector and restorer are available via our website at www.VelocePress.com. We hope that you find this title as interesting as we do.

NOTE FROM THE PUBLISHER

The information presented is true and complete to the best of our knowledge. All recommendations are made without any guarantees on the part of the author or the publisher, who also disclaim all liability incurred with the use of this information.

TRADEMARKS

We recognize that some words, model names and designations, for example, mentioned herein are the property of the trademark holder. We use them for identification purposes only. This is not an official publication.

INFORMATION ON THE USE OF THIS PUBLICATION

This manual is an invaluable resource and a 'must have' for owners interested in performing their own maintenance. However, in today's information age we are constantly subject to changes in common practice, new technology, availability of improved materials and increased awareness of chemical toxicity. As such, it is advised that the user consult with an experienced professional prior to undertaking any procedure described herein. While every care has been taken to ensure correctness of information, it is obviously not possible to guarantee complete freedom from errors or omissions or to accept liability arising from such errors or omissions. Therefore, any individual that uses the information contained within, or elects to perform or participate in do-it-yourself repairs or modifications acknowledges that there is a risk factor involved and that the publisher or its associates cannot be held responsible for personal injury or property damage resulting from the use of the information or the outcome of such procedures.

WARNING!

One final word of advice, this publication is intended to be used as a reference guide, and when in doubt the reader should consult with a qualified technician.

PREFACE

THE Bond Minicar pioneered a new type of motor vehicle, bridging the gap between the motor cycle and the motor car and aiming at the best of two worlds; motor-cycle economy of running (and initial cost) in a car-type body with side-by-side seating and, in fact, all the comfort of a conventional motor car. The Bond Minicar is driven like a car, yet it has a motor-cycle engine with the simplicity of a single-wheel drive. It could be claimed as the modern equivalent of the pony and trap; a very willing mechanical pony developing the power of a dozen "old-fashioned" horses towing a streamlined, modern trap or trailer of stressed-skin construction and designed on similar principles to an aircraft fuselage. The analogy is nearly exact, for the body and engine unit of the Minicar are quite separate entities; the steerable drive unit comprising the engine and front wheel simply being bolted to the main front bulkhead of the body.

The primary idea behind the introduction of the first Minicar was to produce a runabout which could be operated at an absolute minimum of running cost and, at the same time, keep the initial price down by simple construction. Owners of Minicars, however, have proved that the scope of the design is far wider than that. Economy of running remains a primary feature but the Minicar has become as much a "family" car as its "full size" counterpart, with a capacity for two adults and, if needed, two or three children. It has also proved equally at home for continental touring as for daily journeying to work. And it has its adaptation to sporting motoring, through the activities of the Bond Minicar Owners' Club.

The first Bond Minicar Owners' Club was started in Blackburn, Lancs, in 1950 by a small group of enthusiasts; since then some thirty further separate groups have been formed in districts scattered throughout the country. Membership of individual clubs ranges from a dozen or so up to a hundred or more enthusiasts.

The latest Bonds look even more like conventional motor cars than their predecessors. The body has become an enlarged, strengthened unit employing chassis members and the styling has become distinctive and pleasing. On seeing a late model Minicar for the first time one might say not "Look at that three-wheeler!" but "Look at that baby motor car!"

That also introduces another major feature of the Minicar. The layout adopted, with a single front wheel *towing* the car, makes for an extremely stable layout under all driving conditions, especially with the low-slung trailing weight attached. When driving the Minicar, in fact, one soon forgets that it *is* a three-wheeler, for the ride is as safe as—even safer than

PREFACE

—any four-wheeler. And it has powers of manœuvrability that no four-wheeler can give, which can be a particular asset.

The Minicar is not for the fast driver. Its top speed is in the neighbourhood of 45–50 m.p.h., but it will cruise comfortably, and virtually indefinitely, at 40 m.p.h. For week-end driving and, in fact, on most busy roads, average traffic speed is usually of this order; so the Minicar driver can often get from place to place just as quickly as the next fellow in the higher-powered car, and without feeling held back all the time.

Whilst many of the earlier Mark "A" and Mark "B" models continue in regular use the later models offer definite improvements, both in handling qualities and riding comfort. The Mark "C," for example, introduced bonded-rubber rear suspension which has since remained standard on all subsequent models (with an improved type of Flexitor unit introduced later). From the late Mark "C" design, in fact, the mechanical side has remained largely unaltered, although the introduction of a 12-volt electrical system on the Mark "D" was a further substantial improvement.

Whilst coverage of the earlier models up to and including the Mark "D" was complete in the first edition, coverage is now extended to the Mark "E," "F" and "G," the latter becoming the standard production model in 1962 with a twin-cylinder version subsequently introduced in March 1963. Since that date there have been no alterations except for the announcement in 1965 of the Bond "875" which departs radically from the previous Bond formula by employing a Hillman Imp engine and trans-axle assembly.

Not the least virtue of the Minicar is that it is relatively easy and straightforward to maintain, and the self-taught "amateur mechanic" can, indeed, carry out all necessary servicing at home with a minimum of workshop equipment. Even a jack, for example, is unnecessary. Anyone who has the inclination to tackle a motor-cycle engine will find himself equally at home with the Minicar.

This book is essentially practical by nature and covers all the important features of maintenance and servicing as fully as possible. These data are based on standard procedures adopted by Sharp's Commercials Ltd., and draw liberally on their experiences with Minicars over the past decade.

The author would particularly like to express his thanks to Lt. Col. C. R. Gray, Managing Director of Sharp's Commercials Ltd., for facilities extended to visit the works and information provided; and to Messrs. R. Atkinson, R. Hodgkinson, C. Hollings, F. Murphy and J. Woods for their instruction and guidance around the factory. Also to the Villiers Engineering Company Ltd., for supplying data on their engines and permission to reproduce the illustrations in Chapters VI and VIII, and to Raymond Ways for facilities to visit their maintenance shops.

OLD BOSHAM   R. H. WARRING

CONTENTS

CHAP.   PAGE

- I. HISTORY AND DEVELOPMENT 1
- II. OPERATION 7
- III. ROUTINE MAINTENANCE AND LUBRICATION 20
- IV. FAULT FINDING 28
- V. DETAILED MAINTENANCE—
  - Clutch 33
  - Brakes 35
  - Gearbox 39
  - Transmission 39
  - Carburettor 41
  - Decompressor 43
  - Ignition 43
  - Steering 45
  - Rear Suspension 46
  - Wheels and Tyres 46
  - Speedometer Drive 48
  - Decarbonizing 48
  - Body Repairs 49
- VI. VILLIERS 6E AND 8E ENGINES 52
- VII. ELECTRIC SELF-STARTER CONVERSION (6E AND 8E ENGINES) . 59
- VIII. VILLIERS 9E AND 250 C.C. ENGINE 63
- IX. MODIFICATIONS 76
- X. ELECTRICAL EQUIPMENT 87
- XI. DYNASTART UNITS 103

  APPENDIXES—
  - I. *Specifications* 110
  - II. *Modifications* 122
  - III. *Bond Minicar Club* 124
  - *Index* 126

CHAPTER I

HISTORY AND DEVELOPMENT

THE Bond Minicar was originally conceived as a simple runabout aiming at the ultimate in simplicity of construction and economy of operation. It was thought that there was a considerable demand at the time (1948) for such a class of vehicle, which was relatively inexpensive to buy and very cheap to run, for owners to do their shopping, take children to school, and so on; with petrol rationing still in force the 100 miles per gallon performance was an added attraction.

The Bond Minicar is manufactured by Bond Cars Limited of Preston (originally Sharp's Commercials Ltd.), who have continued to develop the design throughout up to the current models. Two factories are operated by the company, one dealing mainly with the manufacture and painting of bodies and the other with fabrication of the remaining components and the actual Minicar assembly line. Engines used throughout are standard Villiers "motor-cycle" type and differ only in minor detail (mainly concerned with the control linkage attachment) from the same engine installed in a motor cycle. Thus maintenance, as far as the engine is concerned, involves essentially "motor cycle" techniques.

The first Bond Minicar appeared in 1948, having undergone some two years' development before this. It was essentially a very austere little car, simple in design and bereft of all luxuries. It was fitted with a "Perspex" windscreen and had no front or rear suspension, the low-pressure balloon tyres fitted being intended to cope with road shocks. The engine used was the Villiers 125 c.c. two-stroke motor-cycle engine which developed a maximum of 5 b.h.p. and gave the Bond a top speed of about 40 m.p.h. and a petrol consumption figure of some 100 miles per gallon. This particular model was designated the Mark "A."

Quite shortly after the first Mark "A" vehicles had been sold it became apparent that their performance and capabilities exceeded the manufacturer's original ideas. One of the first production Mark "A" Bonds, for example, was used by a journalist to take his wife, child and luggage on a continental tour across France and through the Alps: other owners started using Bond Minicars regularly for 200 and 300 mile journeys. In fact, after only twenty-five Mark "A" cars had been produced, it was decided that, as customers were obviously going to use the Minicar for touring abroad or on long journeys at home, the design would benefit from an increase in power. Accordingly an alternative engine, the Villiers 197 c.c. Mark 6E, was made available for the Mark "A." This represented a step-up in power from 5 b.h.p. to 8 b.h.p., increasing the maximum speed to 50–55 m.p.h. and the cruising speed from 30–35 m.p.h. to 40–45 m.p.h. Petrol consumption was only slightly increased, yielding an average performance of 85–95 miles per gallon.

This model was designated the Bond Minicar De Luxe, to distinguish it from the Standard Bond Minicar, the only difference being the engine-gearbox unit. This model continued in production until June, 1951, when the Mark "B" Minicar was introduced, although numerous improvements and modifications were introduced from time to time during this period (as detailed later).

The Bond Minicar Mark "B" retained essentially the same appearance as the Mark "A," with some alteration to the body design to provide sufficient room for an extra seat for a child or additional luggage space. The version fitted with two small seats in the back was offered as an alternative "Family Model."

Other improvements incorporated in the Mark "B" included a curved Triplex glass windscreen, improved front suspension, independent rear suspension and a new type of steering box of rack-and-pinion pattern. The small coil-spring front suspension of the Mark "A" was replaced by a new-type spring and hydraulic shock absorber. The rear suspension was by independent coil-spring units.

The 197 c.c. Villiers 6E engine was retained with the simple form of "pull" starter, consisting of a handle inside the car attached to the kick-starter lever on the engine by a piece of wire; but later, in the same year that the Mark "B" was introduced, a self-starter was offered as an optional extra. This consisted of a starter motor which drove by a Vee-belt on to the flywheel and idled on a freewheel at the side of the flywheel when the engine was running. This also called for a larger battery (6 volt, 57 ampere-hour capacity).

In all, something like 2,000 Mark "A" and 3,000 Mark "B" Minicars were produced up to the end of 1952. In January, 1953, a considerably improved and modified model was introduced as the Mark "C" and was made in greater quantities than any previously produced. Teething troubles which had been apparent throughout the Mark "A" and Mark "B" productions had now been completely overcome, although there were still improvements to follow.

The Bond Minicar Mark "C" had a completely restyled body; independent suspension with the rear wheels mounted on a trailing arm and attached to Flexitor units, which incorporate a central spindle with bonded rubber in tension; three-wheel brakes; and a completely new engine mounting and suspension at the front, the suspension being by trailing arm and coil spring controlled by a hydraulic shock absorber. Worm-and-sector steering also replaced the earlier rack-and-pinion design to give a 90° lock in either direction, literally enabling the car to be turned round in its own diagonal length.

The earlier Mark "C" models retained the Villiers 6E engine but, in July, 1953, this was replaced by the Villiers 8E of the same capacity (but a later development). At the same time a new method of chain adjustment was introduced and some other minor changes incorporated; the facia panel, for example, now extended the full width of the car and eliminated the glove pocket, for which was substituted a handle grip to assist passenger entry and exit, and a manufacturer's motif.

Both the 2-seater and 4-seater Mark "C"s were fitted with a hood as standard, although a moulded Fibreglass hardtop was subsequently made available for "saloon" conversion. On some models Fibreglass construction was also used for the rear wings and bonnet top, although the latter feature was not continued.

Basic model designation continued, as the Standard model with ordinary hand (pull) starting and, in the "De Luxe," with electric starter motor. A truck version was also produced in limited numbers—the Minitruck— with an open truck body. Somewhat previous to this a closed delivery van also had a limited production run—the Minivan—but this was based on the Mark "B" model. Neither of these two commercial class vehicles went into full-scale production and their manufacture was eventually dropped.

The Bond Minicar Mark "D" appeared in May, 1956: it was essentially similar to the Mark "C" but had the Villiers 9E engine (with the SIBA electrical system) with which an optional reverse gear could be provided (of particular benefit to drivers holding a Group "A" licence only), with an improved car-type electrical system (12 volts as opposed to the original 6-volt lighting) and new rear suspension. For the De Luxe model a SIBA electric starter was fitted, consisting of a single unit embodying generator, starter and ignition built into the engine direct on to the crankcase.

Reverse gear, in models fitted with it, is obtained by switching the engine to run in the opposite direction of rotation (accomplished basically by means of a second set of contact points "timed" for opposite-direction firing but with other interior modifications over the standard flywheel magneto unit), the 9E engine running equally well either way. With such a system, of course, a full complement of gearbox ratios is available for driving in reverse, but only first or low gear would be used.

The model "D" was again produced in both 2-seater and 4-seater versions (*see* Fig. 4) with hoods, with a Fibreglass hardtop variant for the 2-seater. The 2-seater Mark "D" ceased production in favour of the Mark "E" when this later model appeared.

A complete change of body design and styling was introduced with the Mark "E," which went into production in December, 1956, overall length being increased by just over a foot, body width also being increased and total weight increasing by a matter of 150 lb due to the different method of construction. The Mark "E" body departs from the original idea of a stressed-skin construction in that it incorporates longitudinal and lateral chassis members of channel-section steel, riveted to 18-gauge aluminium bodywork as one complete unit. The Mark "E" body, in fact, follows modern motor car practice of integral body-chassis construction.

CONSTRUCTIONAL DATA

Model	Body	Front wings	Rear wings	Bonnet	Engine mounting
Mark "A"	18-gauge aluminium	—	18-gauge aluminium	18-gauge aluminium	Unsprung weight
Mark "B"	18-gauge aluminium	—	18-gauge aluminium	18-gauge aluminium	Unsprung weight
Mark "C"	18-gauge aluminium	18-gauge aluminium	18-gauge aluminium or Fibreglass	18-gauge aluminium or Fibreglass	Sprung weight
Mark "D"	18-gauge aluminium	18-gauge aluminium	Fibreglass	18-gauge aluminium	Sprung weight
Mark "E"	Unit-type body-chassis 18-gauge aluminium and steel members	18-gauge aluminium	—	18-gauge aluminium	Sprung weight
Mark "F"	Unit-type body-chassis 18-gauge aluminium and steel members	18-gauge aluminium	—	18-gauge aluminium	Sprung weight
Mark "G"	Unit-type aluminium alloy body with integral steel chassis (glass fibre hardtop)	18-gauge aluminium		18-gauge aluminium	Sprung weight
Model 875 and Ranger 875	Integral type glass-fibre body with integral metal sections	Glass fibre (integral)	Glass fibre (integral)	Glass fibre	Semi-rigid

A further difference introduced with the Mark "E" is the adoption of a four-speed gearbox (four forward speeds), with a reverse drive as an

HISTORY AND DEVELOPMENT

optional extra feature on the same principle adopted with the Mark "D." A Siba "Dynastart" is fitted as standard on either version. The same Villiers 9E engine is employed, but with modified gear ratios.

The Mark "E" is a two-seater, produced with both a hood or a Fibreglass hardtop and represents a "replacement" of the 2-seater Mark "D." There is generous space available in the rear of the body, however, and modification to an alternative four-seater was undertaken during 1958.

This four-seater version, designated the Mark "F" remains virtually identical with the Mark "E" in appearance (and, in fact, utilizes the same hardtop), but it was felt that, to maintain performance with the additional maximum load which might be carried, more power would be helpful. Accordingly, a new 250 c.c. Villiers engine was adopted for the Mark "F," again using a four-speed gearbox (four speeds forward) with reverse optional. The Mark "F" four-seater saloon went into production in early 1959.

With the appearance of the four-seater Mark "F" the four-seater Mark "D" continued in production in its original form except that here also a four-speed gearbox was adopted for the Villiers 9E engine. Thus the later Mark "D" provides an alternative four-seater model with a smaller engine (197 c.c. as against 250 c.c.) and somewhat more economic running at the expense of a slight reduction in performance; although the flexibility of the Mark "D" running with full load is materially improved with the adoption of an additional forward gear.

Main constructional data are summarized in the accompanying table. This may be a useful reference where minor body repairs may have to be tackled, as Fibreglass as well as metal components appears on various models. The use of Fibreglass mouldings is largely restricted to the rear wings on the Mark "D" and some Mark "C"s. Fibreglass was also used on Mark "C" bonnets during a period where aluminium metal was in short supply. All the hardtops are also moulded from Fibreglass, as are the facia panels of the Mark "E" and Mark "F."

The Mark "G", which first appeared in 1962, retained all the main structural and layout features developed through the previous models, but with the 250 c.c. Villiers 35A engine, hydraulic braking, and completely restyled bodywork, as well as other changes of detail. From this date the Mark "G" became the standard production model, commencing with chassis number M/8/40,000, and with three body forms—a four-seat family model or saloon, the Bond Estate, and a van. These three models are designated by the suffix F, E and V, respectively.

A twin-cylinder version of the Mark "G" was subsequently introduced in March 1963, employing the 250 c.c. Villiers Mark 4T two-stroke engine. From this date therefore, the family model, the Estate, and the van have been available with either single- or twin-cylinder engines, differing only in engine installation. Both series are available with either standard Siba Dynastart or reversing Siba Dynastart, giving in effect four versions of the Mark "G" design with three alternative body forms, and have remained unaltered.

The Bond 875 and Ranger 875. The latest model, designated the Bond 875, appeared in prototype form in 1965 and the production version became generally available in 1967. This represents a considerable departure from previous Bond models in that a four-cylinder rear-mounted engine is employed with hypoid bevel drive through rubber and universal-joint couplings to the rear wheels. The engine unit is, in fact, the same as that of the Hillman Imp (Rootes 875 engine) with trans-axle. This gives the Bond 875 an acceleration figure of 0–60 m.p.h. in 16 seconds. This is achieved on standard petrol and at the same time overall fuel consumption for normal driving is of the order of 50 miles per gallon, or better.

The Bond 875 is produced in two versions, a passenger saloon and a van version, known as the Bond Ranger 875. The latter is virtually identical in that the same body shape is preserved, except that the rear-side windows are blanked off and the back is modified for tailgate opening.

The Rootes 875 engine is a four-cylinder overhead camshaft unit, employing largely aluminium alloy die-cast construction for lightness. Bore and stroke are both 2·677 in. (68 mm) giving a cubic capacity of 53·41 cu in. (875 cc). A compression ratio of 8:1 is standard. The engine develops 34 b.h.p. at 4,700 r.p.m. and 47 lb/ft maximum torque at 2,800 r.p.m.

Cooling is by water circulation, employing a centrifugal pump and also assisted by a 9-bladed engine-driven fan. The radiator is pressurized and mounted on the left of the engine. Clutch is a $6\frac{1}{4}$ in. Laycock diaphragm type, hydraulically operated via light foot pressure on the clutch pedal. The gearbox embodies four forward gears and reverse, with synchromesh on all forward gears. A central floor-mounted gearshift lever is fitted with conventional "H" movement (first and third gears "up" and the latter to the right). Reverse is selected by tapping the gear-shift lever to the left from the neutral position and then pulling back.

Suspension differs from the other models since the front wheel is used for steering only. Front suspension comprises a leading arm controlled by a coil spring incorporating a telescopic hydraulic shock-absorber unit. Steering is by a Burman steering box with worm-and-nut operation. Rear suspension is independently sprung, utilizing trailing arms controlled by coil springs and separately attached telescopic hydraulic shock-absorber units. Wheel sizes have been increased all round, now being 12 in. diameter with 5·50 × 12 Michelin "X" tyres fitted as standard.

Since detail maintenance and servicing requirements differ appreciably from those of other models, due to the changed layout, it is impossible to give full coverage for the Bond 875 engine unit, etc., in this present volume. Nevertheless, specific information on the model "875" is included, where relevant or possible, and further useful information will be found in Appendix I.

CHAPTER II

OPERATION

For registration purposes the Bond Minicar is classified as Group G (motor bicycles with or without side-car and tricycles not equipped with means for reversing). This means that a Driving Licence endorsed to cover Vehicle Group G is legally necessary to drive the Minicar, except where the driver holds a provisional licence and displays "L" plates and is accompanied by another person holding a Group G licence.

Many owners who have previously driven cars will probably find that their licence is endorsed for Groups A, B, C and D only, which means that they have to pass a further test for Minicar driving, irrespective of how long they may have held their original licence. This anomalous—and rather stupid—ruling has been overcome in later model Bond Minicars (subsequent to the Mark "C") by offering a reverse gear on the Villiers engine as an optional extra so that holders of licences for Groups A–D only are legally entitled to drive the Minicar without further qualification. The fitting of a reverse gear re-classifies the Minicar as a Group A vehicle.

The basic control layout is essentially similar throughout all models and follows standard motor-car practice in the arrangement of the three foot pedals for accelerator, brake and clutch, respectively, reading from the offside inwards. The handbrake is mounted under the facia on the right, close to the side, and is of the pull or "umbrella handle" type. Additional controls mounted on the floor are a foot-operated bar for the decompressor, a manual start lever (up to Mark "D" models), and a foot-operated dipswitch control on Mark "E" and Mark "F" models.

The facia controls and instruments comprise a centrally-mounted speedometer with mileometer combined as the only standard instrument fitted, together with a choke and various switches and indicators which are dependent on the model concerned. A second-hand Minicar, particularly of an early type, may have a number of non-standard fittings, e.g. some original owners may have fitted an ammeter to read charge and discharge rates, non-standard switches in various positions (controlling, for example, self-installed trafficator systems), modified lighting, controls for a self-starter conversion, and so on. The following descriptions therefore apply only to the various models in their standard or original form.

A drawing of the facia panel of the Mark "A" is shown in Fig. 1. The choke control (pull-out knob) is mounted on the left-hand side of the speedometer with the light switch on the right-hand side under the wheel.

The light switch is of the toggle type, "up" for headlamps and "down" for sidelights. The only other facia controls are the toggle-type ignition switch on the extreme right and the horn button immediately beneath it.

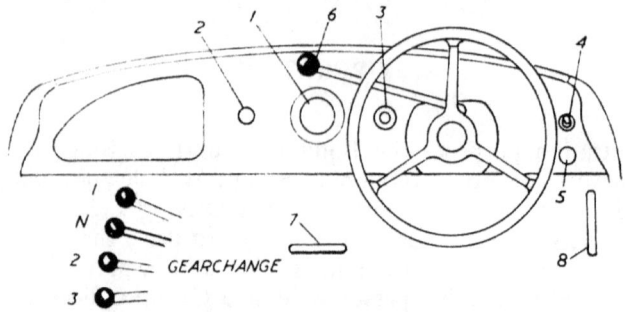

Fig. 1. Mark "A" Facia

Windscreen wiper on original model was manually operated; electric wiper a later addition.

1. Speedometer
2. Choke
3. Head-sidelight switch
4. Ignition switch
5. Horn button
6. Gear-change lever
7. Decompressor (foot-operated)
8. Handbrake

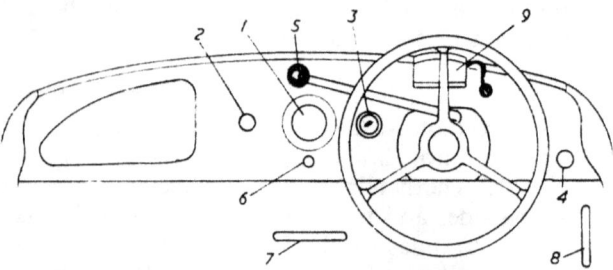

Fig. 2. Mark "B" Facia and Controls

1. Speedometer
2. Choke
3. Ignition (key) and light switch
4. Horn button
5. Gear-change lever
6. Dash light switch
7. Decompressor (foot-operated)
8. Handbrake
9. Electric wiper motor

The windscreen wiper is manually operated, although an electric motor type was also fitted.

The gear-change lever is mounted on the same top bracket as the steering-wheel bearing, the three gear positions and neutral being indicated on the diagram. Floor-mounted controls comprise the handbrake on the extreme right, the three foot pedals, the decompressor well to the left of the clutch and the pull-type manual starter.

The Mark "B" facia is shown in Fig. 2. An electric windscreen wiper is now fitted as standard, mounted on top of the facia above the wheel.

OPERATION

The ignition switch is moved inwards and is now of the key type incorporated in the light switch (turn to the right for headlights, and to the left for sidelights). The horn button remains in the same position, also the choke, but an additional switch is fitted under the speedometer to operate the dash light. The floor controls follow essentially the same pattern as those on the Mark "A."

The early Mark "C" Minicars retained the same form of facia panel with a cut-out glove pocket on the offside. Many of the controls are, however, repositioned. The combined light and ignition switch is moved to underneath the speedometer and the panel light to the right. The horn button comes in the centre of the steering wheel with a dip switch for the

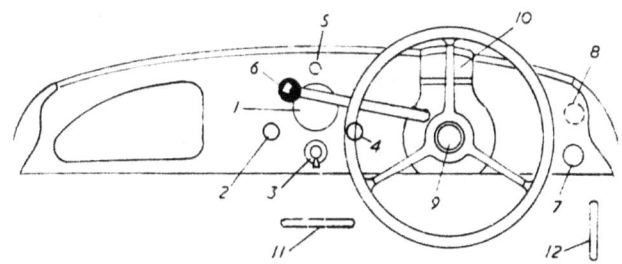

Fig. 3. Early Mark "C" Facia and Controls

When a self-starter is fitted the charge rate control is eliminated.

1. Speedometer
2. Choke
3. Ignition (key) and light switch
4. Panel light switch
5. Charge rate control
6. Gear-change lever
7. Dip switch
8. Starter (on self-starter models)
9. Horn button
10. Wiper motor
11. Decompressor
12. Handbrake

lights taking its original position on the right-hand side (Fig. 3). If the particular model was adapted to the higher output generator the charge-rate control switch (push-pull type) then appeared over the centre of the speedometer.

The glove compartment was eliminated from the facia on later Mark "C"s (from the time of fitting the Villiers 8E engine) and a grip handle and badge mounted on the facia at this side. Otherwise the controls followed an identical layout except in the De Luxe version with self-starter. Here the starter switch is mounted on the right-hand side above the dip switch. The fitting of a starter eliminates the need for charge-rate control and so this switch is no longer fitted with a starter. A manual start Mark "C" with the 8E engine would, however, have an identical layout *with* the charge-rate control switch retained but the starter switch eliminated.

Fig. 4 shows the facia panel of the Mark "D" standard model, retaining essentially the same grouping again. As with the Mark "C," the fitting of a self-starter brings a starter switch, fitted on the right-hand side of the wheel, and eliminates the charge-rate control switch.

The Mark "D" is also available with reverse gear, reverse being obtained by electrical switching to make the engine run in the opposite direction

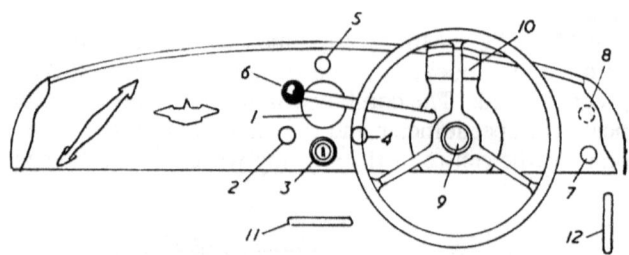

FIG. 4. STANDARD MARK "D" FACIA AND CONTROLS

5. Charge rate control (becomes ignition warning lamp on self-starter model). (For other numbered annotations *see* Fig. 3.)

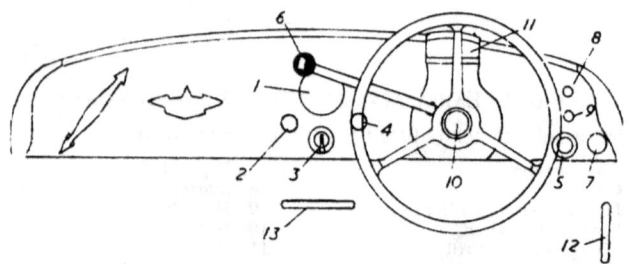

FIG. 5. MARK "D" WITH REVERSE

3. Light switch only
4. Panel light
5. Ignition and starter (key)
8, 9. Ignition warning lights (one light on, forward drive selected; both lights, reverse)

10. Horn button
11. Wiper motor
13. Decompressor

(For other numbered annotations *see* Fig. 3)

to normal. The main control group remains the same as in the Mark "C" and "D" Standard except that the combined ignition and starter switch is isolated from the light switch and re-located on the right-hand side of the wheel. Above this switch are two red indicator lamps (*see* Fig. 5).

The combined ignition and starter switch operates as a two-position control. Switching on (clockwise) switches on the ignition. A continued turn in the same direction operates the starter motor. For reverse, the key is *depressed* and turned clockwise to ignition and through to start. When forward position is selected, switching on the ignition illuminates *one* red indicator light. If the key is depressed and switched to *reverse* position *both* indicator lights are illuminated. These lights, therefore, positively identify whether forward or reverse drive is operating.

The 1959 Mark "D" incorporates a four-speed gearbox. The gear-change handle is still mounted on the steering head but the selection of gears operates indirectly on a sequence position. The movement is shown in Fig. 6. An additional *green* indicator lamp is fitted to the dash which lights up when the ignition is switched on and *neutral* gear is selected. This is a very useful indicator since it is not possible to tell from the position of the gear lever which gear is actually engaged, the lever always being in the horizontal position in *any* gear *and* in neutral.

Starting from neutral and changing *up*, first gear is selected by moving the gear lever upwards and back again to the horizontal position, bearing

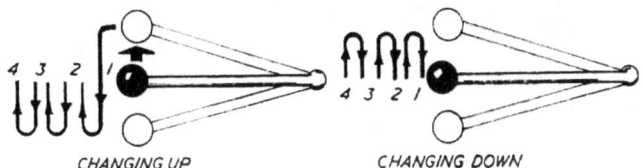

CHANGING UP   CHANGING DOWN

Fig. 6. Change Movements on the Four-speed Gearbox

Changing up, slight downward pressure must be applied between first and neutral. Changing down apply slight upward pressure from second to neutral.

down lightly on the gear lever on the return stroke. Second gear is selected by pulling the gear lever down and back again. Repeating this movement engages third gear, and repeating it again fourth gear. Third gear can only be reached *through* second, and fourth gear *through* third, although first or second can be selected direct from neutral.

To change *down* the lever is moved upwards and back again. Each movement changes one gear at a time, e.g. fourth to third, then third to second, then second to first, then, moving the lever downwards, first to neutral. From second gear down to neutral *slight* upward pressure is required on the gear lever.

It is particularly important in all changes to ensure that the gear lever is returned to the *horizontal* position before engaging the next gear.

Control group of the four-speed Mark "D" is shown in Fig. 7, the two indicator lamps being mounted above the speedometer. The red lamp is the ignition warning light and the green lamp the neutral indicator for the four-speed gear change. In the case of the Mark "D" with four-speed gearbox and Dynastart reverse only the neutral indicator lamp is positioned above the speedometer and the two ignition warning lamps are set to the right (Fig. 8). These work on the same principle as described for the three-speed model: one light on indicates forward drive selected; two lights on, reverse drive.

Fig. 7. Controls and Facia Mark "D" with Four-speed Gearbox

1. Speedometer
2. Choke
3. Ignition and light switch
4. Panel light
5. Starter
6. Dip switch
7. Ignition warning lamp (red)
8. Neutral indicator lamp (green)
9. Gear-change lever
10. Horn button
11. Handbrake

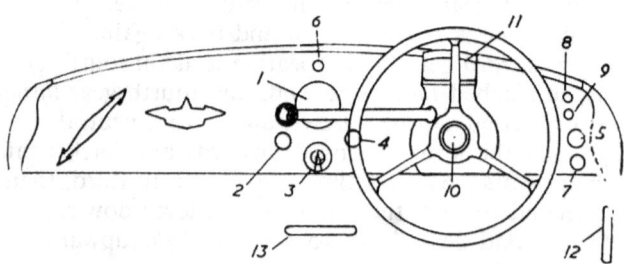

Fig. 8. Mark "D" Model with Four-speed Gearbox and Reverse

1. Speedometer
2. Choke
3. Light switch
4. Panel light
5. Ignition and starter (key)
6. Neutral indicator lamp (green)
7. Dip switch
8, 9. Red indicator lamps (one forward; both reverse)
10. Horn button
11. Wiper motor
12. Handbrake
13. Decompressor

OPERATION

The Mark "E" and Mark "F" models represent a considerable difference in styling. A large shelf extends across the full width of the body and the facia panel is a separate Fibreglass moulding mounted on the right-hand side (Fig. 9). A four-speed gearbox is standard on these models, the gear change being as described above. Also either model is available with or without Dynastart reverse. The only difference lies in the provision of

Fig. 9. Mark "E" and Mark "F" Facia and Controls

1. Speedometer
2. Panel light
3. Choke
4. Lights (pull for side; turn and pull again for head)
5. Wiper switch
6. Ignition and starter
7. Ignition warning light (red)
8. Neutral indicator light (green)
9. Gear-change lever (four-speed gearbox)
10. Trafficator switch (winking lights—light in centre of this switch acts as an indicator to driver)
11. Handbrake

Horn button is in centre of steering wheel

(A small light acts as an indicator to headlamp position, coming on in the high beam position when the headlights are switched on.)

twin red indicator lamps in the case of the reverse model. Fig. 10 details the Mark "E" and Mark "F" controls, which are identical for these two marks.

Other differences from all the earlier models are the inclusion of a trafficator control as standard (winking lights controlled by a switch on the right-hand side), a pull-type light switch (first pull out for side lights, rotate slightly clockwise and pull again for headlights), and a foot-operated dip switch on the floor approximately in the centre and near the left bulkhead.

The other controls of significance for operation are concerned with the petrol supply; the fuel tap is fitted at the bottom of the petrol tank and the carburettor "tickler" used to ensure that the carburettor float chamber is full of fuel for starting.

The fuel tap on Marks "A" and "B" is accessible from inside the car underneath the scuttle. On Marks "C," "D," "E" and "F" models the tap comes on the outside of the bulkhead immediately underneath the petrol tank platform, and is accessible from beneath the bonnet.

The main switch is of the push-pull type with "on" and "off" positions marked on the face of the slide. The tap may be at various angles, depending on how it was screwed in position, but should face fore-and-aft, pushing backwards for "on" and pulling out for "off." The reserve

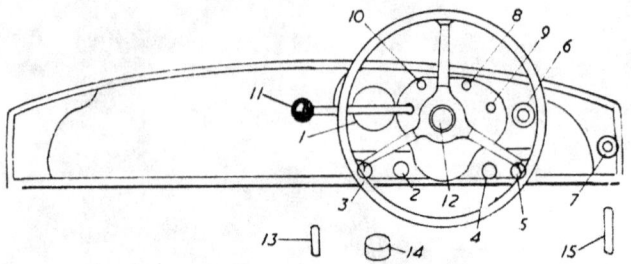

Fig. 10. Mark "E" and Mark "F" with Reverse Drive

1. Speedometer
2. Choke
3. Panel light
4. Lights
5. Wiper
6. Ignition and starter (key)
7. Trafficator switch (winking lights)
8, 10. Red indicator lamps (one for forward; two for reverse)
9. Neutral indicator lamp (green)
11. Gear-change lever
12. Horn button
13. Decompressor
14. Dip switch (foot operated)
15. Handbrake

switch is a small lever mounted in the same body above the slide and at right-angles to it. The reserve position is marked, but its setting can be memorized as being in the extreme anti-clockwise position (viewed from above) for normal operation and being rotated to the extreme clockwise position to switch on to reserve fuel supply. This tap works on the simple principle of providing an escape path for fuel in the bottom of the tank below the level of the feed pipe entering the tank (which projects above the tank bottom).

The reserve switch should always be kept in the normal position so that, should the occasion arise when you do run out of petrol on the road, it can be switched on to the reserve position to give further running time to get to the nearest filling station, or home. The approximate running time on reserve tank capacity only is a matter of some 20 miles. The main fuel tap should normally be switched to the "off" position on completion of

OPERATION

a run, and should always be switched off if the car is to be left standing for a considerable period.

The carburettor "tickler" control (*see* Fig. 22) is simply a spring-loaded plunger which depresses the float in the carburettor and allows the float chamber to fill with fuel ready for starting. It should only be depressed until fuel begins to run from the top of the carburettor. Operation of the tickler is usually necessary to prime the carburettor after the engine has been standing idle for some time, and nearly always for starting from cold in cold weather.

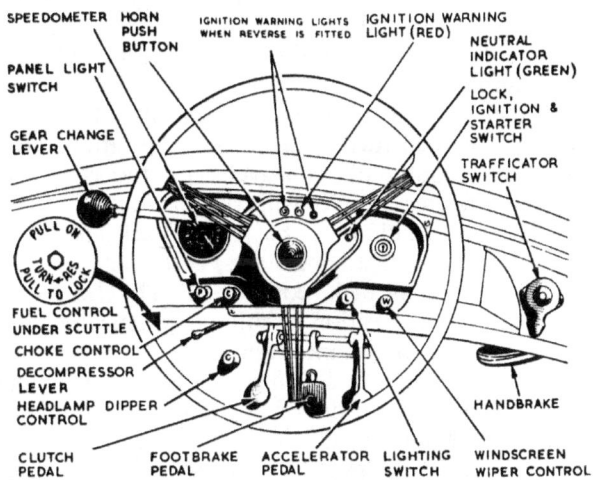

FIG. 11. INSTRUMENTS AND CONTROLS MARK "G"

Instrument and control layout of the Mark "G" (*see* Fig. 11) is basically similar to that of the Mark "E," but with the fuel control tap under the scuttle. "On," "Off" and "Reserve" positions are marked on the end of the control rod, the action being "pull" for "On" and "turn" (clockwise) for "Reserve."

The fuel mixture specified for the Villiers engine is a 16:1 petrol-oil mixture, the addition of oil providing lubrication for the moving parts in the engine. It is *absolutely essential* that a petrol-oil mixture of the correct ratio be *always* used, as serious damage can result to the engine through lack of lubrication if run on insufficient oil. For the same reason the oil used should be to the maker's specification—SAE 30/40.

If oil and petrol are added separately to the tank the fuel tap should be turned off and the oil added first. This gives optimum mixing when the petrol is poured in on top. If petrol is poured first into an empty tank there is a possibility of the initial supply to the carburettor being neat petrol so that the engine is starved of oil when first running. If the fuel tap is left on and oil added first, there is a possibility of filling the fuel line to the carburettor with neat oil so that the engine will not start simply because it is getting only lubricating oil through.

Special two-stroke oils have enhanced mixing power and will generally mix satisfactorily, irrespective of whether the oil or petrol is added first to the tank. They are coming more into favour and most garages now include such supplies, generally with special oil dispensers. The old standard of a good SAE 30 engine oil to mix with petrol is, however, just as satisfactory.

Starting Technique (Manual Start). For starting, the front wheel should always be pointing straight ahead and the gear lever must be in the neutral position. The fuel tap is turned to the "on" position and the carburettor tickler operated until petrol is just beginning to flood from the top of the carburettor. The choke control is pulled out to its fullest extent.

The ignition key is then turned to the "on" position, the accelerator pedal depressed to about half its travel with the right foot and the decompressor pedal depressed fully with the left foot.

The starting handle should then be pulled back sharply to spin the engine over. As soon as the engine starts, ease back on the accelerator and release the decompressor pedal completely. The choke control should also be returned to the off position as soon as practicable, i.e. as soon as this can be done without the engine stopping.

That is the basic principle of starting. Individual technique will vary slightly. The best starting position for the accelerator pedal, for example, will vary with different engines and is only established on a "trial and error" basis. Also, early Mark "A" models retain the original direct-acting decompressor, which must be *released* towards the end of each pull, or alternatively the engine pulled over a number of times slowly with the decompressor operated and then (to start) sharply *with the decompressor released* (the first Mark "A" models with 125-c.c. engines had no decompressor).

The engine should start within four to six pulls on the handle. If not, further pulling will probably make matters worse. The usual cause of bad starting (apart from deterioration in the case of an old engine) is flooding or too much fuel drawn into the cylinder, wetting the plug and preventing it from sparking. The cure in such cases is to switch the ignition off, turn off the fuel, hold the decompressor pedal down and pull the engine over smartly a number of times to blow the excess fuel out of the exhaust and so clear the engine. If the flooding is bad it may be necessary to remove the spark plug as well before carrying out the above and dry the plug thoroughly before replacing it.

Excessive use of the carburettor "tickler" can result in almost immediate flooding. It may only be necessary, in fact, to use the tickler in cold weather. Again this is a feature which will depend to a large extent on the individual characteristics of the engine. Use of the tickler should certainly not be required to start an engine which is still warm, nor should the choke control be used in such circumstances.

If the engine proves difficult to start when hot, almost certainly again the cause is flooding and the spark plug will have to be removed and the engine cleared, as described above. With bad flooding—the plug appearing very wet—it will assist matters if the crankcase drain plug is also removed, (*see* Fig. 12) to clear excess mixture which has gathered in the bottom of the engine.

Other possible causes of bad starting are a dirty spark plug or faulty ignition. These points can be checked and rectified as described in Chapters III and IV.

The Minicar is driven like any conventional motor car. The stability is extremely good and the steering is light and responsive, the later models especially having first-class handling qualities. Another favourable feature is the extreme manœuvrability. The 90-degree lock given by the worm-and-sector steering adopted from the Mark "C" onwards means that the Minicar may be driven off at right angles from a facing obstruction as well as making it far more manœuvrable in traffic than a conventional motor car (where its small size is a further advantage). A point which Minicar drivers might well bear in mind, however, is that they may not be visible to drivers of a larger car when approaching it diagonally from the left, the other driver's vision being obscured by the nearside windscreen pillar and the low silhouette of the Minicar running, close up, below his line of vision.

Brakes are quite satisfactory within the normal performance range of the Minicar, provided they are kept in good adjustment. Braking power is appreciably better on the later models than the Mark "A" and Mark "B" which had rear wheel brakes. If the brakes are applied excessively hard there may be some tendency for the rear of the car to bounce, unless weighted down.

Roll on cornering is negligible. If cornered too fast the back wheels can be made to slide but in general the single tractor front wheel is of considerable help in maintaining control under difficult conditions, literally tugging the vehicle out of trouble with a little acceleration. Driving technique thus does differ from standard car practice, but can be put to full advantage once mastered.

Good driving technique requires full use of the gears. It will require a certain amount of practice to master snappy gear changes, particularly first to second where the gear lever has to be brought back through neutral—top gear may be selected accidentally. With the four-speed gearbox models the sequence control may prove tricky at first but again resolves itself as an automatic action with practice.

With the three-speed gearbox the Minicar can be driven up to about 18–20 m.p.h. in first although the normal point for changing up would be 10–12 m.p.h. Absolute maximum speed in second gear is of the order

Fig. 12 (*a*). Gearbox filler (1), and dipstick (2) on earlier engines. Level plug (3) and gearbox drain plug (4).

Fig. 12 (*b*). Combined filler and dipstick position on 9E engines arrowed. The position of the level and drain plugs varies slightly on three-speed and four-speed models.

of 30–35 m.p.h., but the change would normally be made between 22 and 28 m.p.h. Maximum speed in top is of the order of 45–50 m.p.h. The above change figures apply to maximum acceleration through gears (although this will vary slightly with different models and the condition of the vehicle) when top speed should be reached in about 45 seconds, For normal driving both first and second gear changes may be made somewhat earlier.

The engine should never be allowed to labour in any gear, and one should change down to a lower gear on inclines, etc. Nor should the Minicar be driven slowly in top gear. The engine will begin to snatch in top gear when slowed to about 20 m.p.h. and a change down should always be made before this occurs.

Another point about driving is that letting the engine idle or run slowly for long periods may foul up the plug, so under such conditions an occasional touch on the accelerator is advisable. When idling with no forward speed, there may also be a tendency for the engine to overheat.

For running-in purposes, the manufacturers recommend that the following road speeds should not be exceeded for the first 500 miles.

Three-speed gearbox	1st gear	10 m.p.h.
	2nd gear	15 m.p.h.
	3rd gear (top)	25 m.p.h.
Four-speed gearbox	1st gear	8 m.p.h. (10 m.p.h. Mark F)
(Models D & E)	2nd gear	13 m.p.h. (15 m.p.h. ,,)
	3rd gear	18 m.p.h. (20 m.p.h. ,,)
	4th gear (top)	28 m.p.h. (30 m.p.h. ,,)
Four-speed gearbox	1st gear	10 m.p.h.
(Mark "G" single-	2nd gear	15 m.p.h.
cylinder engine)	3rd gear	20 m.p.h.
	4th gear (top)	30 m.p.h.
Four-speed gearbox	1st gear	8 m.p.h.
(Mark "G" twin-	2nd gear	15 m.p.h.
cylinder engine)	3rd gear	25 m.p.h.
	4th gear (top)	35 m.p.h.

During the first 200 miles or so of the engine life it is also helpful to increase the proportion of oil in the fuel for extra lubrication. A new engine will also lack power, but performance will progressively improve as high spots are worn off and the running parts become bedded down. Considerable damage can be done by overworking the engine during this period or from insufficient lubrication but, if carefully run-in, maximum performance should be achieved by 500–1,000 miles, and the engine completely settled down by 2,000 miles.

CHAPTER III

ROUTINE MAINTENANCE AND LUBRICATION

REGULAR maintenance is an essential feature for the well-being of any piece of machinery, particularly in respect of keeping all working parts properly lubricated and everything in correct adjustment. Lubrication minimizes wear and friction, making for both a longer life and better performance of all the parts concerned. Periodic adjustments not only make for better handling characteristics but also reduce wear and maintain performance.

The moving parts of the Villiers engine as fitted to all Bond Minicars are lubricated internally by oil mixed with the petrol. The recommended petrol-oil proportion is 20:1 (or 16:1 where two-stroke mixing oil is used) and this ratio should always be kept constant. The dangers of economizing on oil in the mixture have already been stressed. On the other hand, an excess of oil, which makes the mixture more expensive, may provide better lubrication but this will be in excess of normal running requirements. In other words, the excess proportion of oil is not doing any useful work and so is wasted. At the same time it is lowering the performance of the engine by reducing the petrol content of the fuel and it also makes for sluggish starting.

The only time to use an excess of oil in the mixture is with a brand-new engine when it will be a safeguard to use a fuel mixture of about 12:1 petrol-oil for the first 200–250 miles of the engine's life. After that the standard 16:1 mixture can be used throughout the rest of the life of the engine.* It will not pay to continue running too long with an excess of oil in the mixture as this will tend to form sooty deposits inside the engine which will detract from performance and may call for early decarbonizing.

Any departure from the recommended oil viscosity (SAE 30/40) is also to be avoided. A thinner oil (lower SAE number) may lack the required lubricating properties or break down under the engine heat. A thicker oil (higher SAE number) may not mix adequately with the petrol and tend to separate out in the tank. Any marked departure from the standard mixture, too, will tend to affect the carburettor settings and adjustment.

The gears and primary chain drive receive independent lubrication by virtue of running in an oil bath; i.e. these units being enclosed, the gearbox and chain case are both filled to the required level and the oil kept at a suitable level by topping-up from time to time (at regular intervals). A heavy gear oil (SAE 140) is specified for the 6E and 8E

* See lubrication table (pages 25–7) for complete information.

engines for both gearbox and chain case, but a much lighter oil for the 9E engine, viz.—

	Gearbox	Chain Case
Mark "D" and "E" Minicar . .	SAE 30	SAE 20

Mark "F" and Mark "G" Specification similar

The oil level in the gearbox is readily checked by means of the dipstick (*see* Fig. 12). The positions of the filler plug, level plug, and drain plug are also illustrated on this view. The latter is for draining off all the oil from

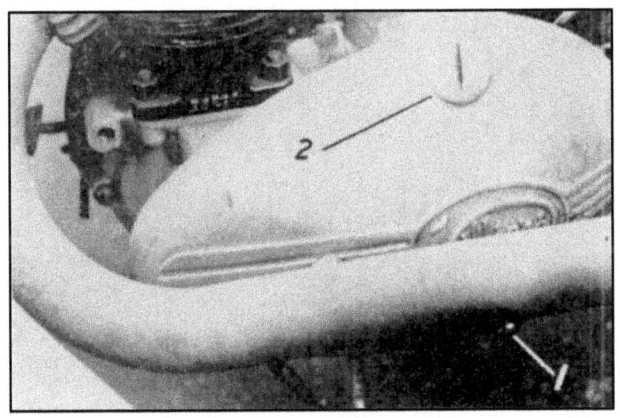

Fig. 13 (*a*). Primary Chain Case
Level plug (1) and filler plug (2) on chain case (similar on all engines).

the gearbox when required (e.g. for a complete oil change). For normal maintenance the oil level is merely topped-up through the filler plug to the required level as indicated by the dipstick. When refilling the gearbox it is usually easiest to remove the dipstick entirely for better access to the filler.

The primary chain case is on the other (left) side of the engine, fitted with a filler plug and level plug (*see* Fig. 13 (*a*)). The correct level of oil is established by removing the level plug and topping-up through the filler plug until oil just begins to overflow from the level plug. Both plugs are then replaced. A separate drain plug is not necessary for the primary chain case since if the oil is to be drained completely the whole cover can be removed.

Other lubricating points are covered by grease nipples or points to be greased or oiled independently. The location of these is illustrated in Fig. 14 and the reference numbers given apply throughout the regular maintenance tables which follow.

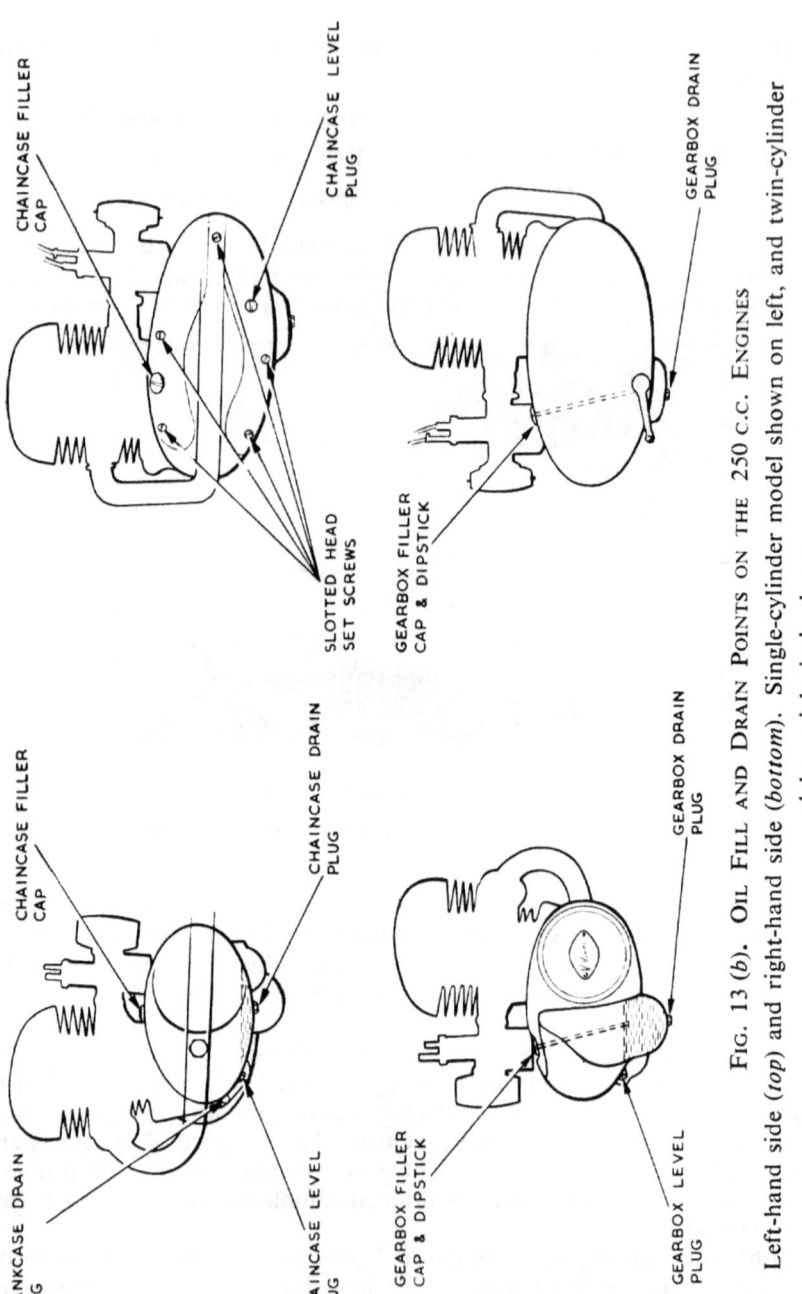

FIG. 13 (b). OIL FILL AND DRAIN POINTS ON THE 250 C.C. ENGINES Left-hand side (*top*) and right-hand side (*bottom*). Single-cylinder model shown on left, and twin-cylinder model on right in both cases.

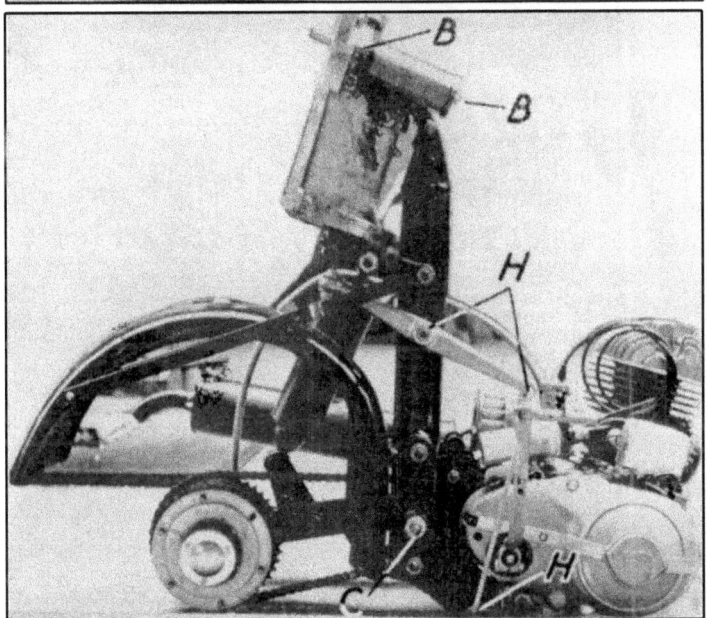

Fig. 14. Lubrication Points on the 9E Engine Unit

References *A*, *B*, etc., apply to maintenance table. Note that the approximate position of the cable grease points is indicated although the cables themselves are not shown in this illustration.

REGULAR ROUTINE MAINTENANCE

Period	Check or action	Position ref. (Fig. 14)	Lubricant and/or remarks
Weekly	(i) Check tyre pressures		*See* tyre pressures data
	(ii) Check fuel level in tank (at shorter intervals if driving more than 200 miles per week)		Refill, as necessary, making sure that reserve tap is in normal position after refilling
	(iii) Check electrolyte level in battery		Top-up with distilled water, as necessary, until plates are just covered
Lubrication— Every 500 miles or 3 weeks	Apply grease gun to the following lubrication points (grease nipples)		Any good quality automobile grease can be used
	(i) Steering-head spindle	A	One nipple in centre of steering-head bracket
	(ii) Steering-worm shaft bearings	B	One nipple at each end of housing
	(iii) Front trailing-arm bearings	C	At pivot point
	(iv) Front brake camshaft	D	Nipple at end of shaft
	(v) Rear brake camshaft	—	Nipple on underside of trailing arm
	(vi) Handbrake cable	—	Nipple in centre of cable (near bulkhead)
	(vii) Front brake cable	E	Nipple in centre of cable (on mudguard)
	(viii) Clutch cable		Nipple in centre of cable
	The following should be smeared with grease		Use good quality automobile grease
	(i) Steering sector teeth	F	
	(ii) Steering worm	G	
	The following points should be oiled		Use good quality machine and an oil-can
	(i) Gear lever bearing		On facia panel
	(ii) Gear lever linkage (*not* rubber bushes)	H	
	(iii) Starter lever fulcrum bearing	—	Inside body on floor
	(iv) Starter cable	—	Where it emerges from sheath
	(v) Clutch and accelerator pedal spindle	—	
	(vi) Decompressor pedal spindle	—	
	(vii) Brake-adjustment nuts and trunnions	—	
	(viii) Brake cross-shaft bearings	—	Under floor by bottom edge of bulkhead
	(ix) Brake-rod lever linkages	—	Under body (*see* Fig. 18)
	(x) Engine-torque reaction linkage	—	

ROUTINE MAINTENANCE AND LUBRICATION

Period	Check or action	Lubricant and/or remarks
Maintenance— Every 500 miles or 3 weeks	Check wheel nuts Clean primary-drive chain by wiping down and lubricate by smearing on graphited grease Check chain adjustment Clean spark plug	Tighten, if necessary If very dirty, remove and clean Readjust tension, if necessary —
Lubrication and Maintenance— Every 1,000 miles or 6 weeks	Repeat 500-mile check Check oil level in gearbox Check oil level in chain case Clean and check spark-plug gap	 Top-up with oil as necessary (see table of lubricants) Top-up to level plug with SAE 140, 30 or 20, as appropriate Readjust gap to 0·018 in.–0·025 in., if necessary
Lubrication and Maintenance— Every 5,000 miles or 6 months	Drain gearbox oil and refill (see Fig. 12) Drain and refill chain case (see Fig. 13) Remove and clean chain Repack wheel-hub bearings Check and adjust clutch Check and adjust brakes Check carburettor Clean air filter Check contact-breaker Check steering-head spindle Check steering worm-shaft Decarbonize engine, if necessary	Remove filler and drain plugs to drain. Wipe plugs clean before replacing Detach chain case to drain Clean chain in paraffin, wipe dry and grease thoroughly before replacing Remove hub caps, pack with grease and replace These items may, of course, already have been attended to at a previous check Remove carburettor, strip and clean Remove air filter, wash in petrol, dry soak in clean oil before replacing Remove flywheel cover, clean and check points, readjusting gap, as necessary (0·015 in. gap correct) Tighten, if necessary Adjust, if necessary No definite rule can be given as to when decarbonizing is necessary since this depends on the type of petrol and oil, how the engine is driven, etc. (see Chapter V, Section 12)

TYRE PRESSURE DATA

Mark "A": front 16* lb/in.², rear 12† lb/in.²
Mark "B": front 24 lb/in.², rear 18 lb/in.²
Mark "C" and "D": front 28 lb/in.², rear 22 lb/in.²
Mark "E" and "F": front 36 lb/in.², rear 22–24 lb/in.²
Mark "G": front 36 lb/in.²
rear 24 lb/in.² (two persons)
30 lb/in.² (fully loaded)
875 and Ranger 875: front 22 lb/in.²
rear 24 lb/in.² or 26 lb/in.² (fully loaded)

* Increase to 20 lb/in.² with hydraulic shock absorber.
† Increase to 22 lb/in.² with "Flexitor" rear suspension.

LUBRICANT TABLE—VILLIERS 6E AND 8E ENGINES

(Bond Minicars Mark "A," Mark "B" and Mark "C")

The previous table (page 25) applies *except for oil specification for gearbox and chain case.*

	SHELL	BP	ESSO	MOBIL	WAKEFIELD	DUCKHAMS
Gearbox and chain case (SAE 140)	Spirax 140	Energol SAE 140	Esso Gear Oil 140	Mobilube C	Castrol D	Duckhams N2 Gear Oil

LUBRICANT TABLE—VILLIERS 35A (single-cylinder) AND MARK "4T" (twin-cylinder) ENGINES

(All Bond Mark "G" Models)

	BP	DUCKHAMS	ESSO	MOBIL	SHELL	WAKEFIELD	E. JOYS
Engine* (1) Petrol/Oil ratio 20:1 unless otherwise stated	Energol Two Stroke Petroiler Mix or Energol Two Stroke Oil	Nol Thirty or Duckhams Two Stroke Oil	Esso Two Stroke Motor Oil (16:1) or Essolube 30	MobilMix TT (16:1) or Mobiloil A	Shell 2T Mixture or Shell 2T Two Stroke Oil	Castrol Two-Stroke Oil (16:1) or Castrol XL	Filtrate (32:1)
(2) Petrol/Oil ratio 16:1 unless otherwise stated	Energol Two Stroke Oil	Nol Thirty or Duckhams Two Stroke Oil (12:1)	Esso Two Stroke Motor Oil (12:1) or Essolube 30	MobilMix TT (12:1) or Mobiloil A	Shell 2T Two Stroke Oil	Castrol Two Stroke Oil (12:1) or Castrol XL	Filtrate (24:1)
Gearbox	Energol SAE 30	Nol Thirty	Essolube 30	Mobiloil A	Shell X-100 30	Castrol XL	Filtrate Medium 30
Chaincase	SAE 5	SAE 5	SAE 5	SAE 5	SAE 5	Castrol TQ SAE 5	SAE 5
Grease Points	Energrease L2	Duckhams LB 10 Grease	Esso Multi-Purpose Grease H	Mobilgrease MP	Retinax A	Castrolease LM	Filtrate Super Lithium Grease

* Use grades recommended against (2) for engines during first 1,000 miles

LUBRICANT TABLE—VILLIERS 9E ENGINE §
(Bond Minicars Mark "D," Mark "E" and Mark "F")
(Recommended proprietary lubricants)

	SHELL	BP	ESSO	MOBIL	CASTROL	DUCKHAMS
Engine oil (20 : 1* ratio)	SHELL TT or SHELL 2T	ENERGOL TWO-STROKE OIL or ENERGOL TWO-STROKE PETROILER MIX	ESSO TWO-STROKE OIL	MOBILMIX TT or MOBILOIL A†	CASTROL TWO-STROKE OIL† or CASTROL XL	NOL THIRTY or DUCKHAMS TWO-STROKE OIL
Engine oil (16 : 1 ratio)	SHELL 2T	ENERGOL TWO-STROKE OIL	ESSO TWO-STROKE OIL or ESSOLUBE 30	MOBILMIX TT or MOBILOIL A‡	CASTROL TWO-STROKE OIL or CASTROL XL‡	NOL THIRTY or DUCKHAMS TWO-STROKE OIL
Gearbox oil (SAE 30)	X-100 30	ENERGOL SAE 30	ESSOLUBE 30	MOBILOIL A	CASTROL XL	NOL THIRTY
Chain case oil (SAE 20)	X-100 20/20W	ENERGOL SAE 20W	ESSOLUBE 20	MOBILOIL ARCTIC	CASTROLITE	NOL TWENTY
Grease points	RETINAX A	ENERGREASE L2	ESSO GREASE H	MOBILGREASE MP	CASTROLEASE LM	LB 10 GREASE

* Not recommended for the first 1,000 miles running of a new engine. (Use 16 : 1 ratio.)
† Adjust petrol oil ratio to 16 : 1.   ‡ Adjust petrol oil ratio to 12 : 1.
§ For lubricants for "875" and "Ranger 875" models see page 121.

CHAPTER IV

FAULT FINDING

MOST of the minor or apparent faults which may develop are more often than not due to "owner error" rather than to the mechanical system involved, either in not appreciating what is being done wrong (e.g. excessive choking, resulting in the spark plug becoming too wet to fire), or in ignoring *necessary* maintenance items, particularly lubrication, so that a part or cable seizes-up or prematurely fails. Even the simplest and most obvious of faults like running out of petrol can be baffling—and most frustrating—to an owner-driver who, although perhaps an experienced *driver*, has never troubled to master even the rudiments of how his car operates.

Whilst the earlier model Minicars (Marks "A" and "B") suffered from certain inherent weaknesses (basically the changes detailed in Chapter IX cover such features), all subsequent models have proved relatively trouble-free when *properly maintained*. The secret is, of course, in this emphasis on regular maintenance.

The Minicar engine is called upon to do a considerable amount of hard work, which in itself is no limitation, for a good two-stroke engine thrives on such treatment so long as it is kept in good condition. It is also a single-cylinder engine which, necessarily, is subject to more vibration than a multi-cylinder car engine although in many respects it is called upon to do a car engine's duty. Once anything starts to get out of adjustment, therefore, its ultimate failure can be accelerated by neglect.

For a new Minicar, the first 2,000 miles are fairly critical, governing its behaviour over the rest of its life; and the first 500 miles are the most critical of all.

The following tables are designed to locate typical faults against probable causes, and their cure. Where a major fault is involved, of course, putting the trouble right may involve more than simple action. In such cases more detailed information can be found in Chapter III on Maintenance, under specific headings, or in Chapters VI and VIII describing the engine units in detail. Most of the simpler faults can, however, be dealt with by the owner on the spot, or at least in his garage, without incurring the service charges made for professional attention.

FAULT FINDING

Trouble or Symptom(s)	Possible cause	Remedy
1. Engine will not turn over when starter is pulled (manual start)	(i) Clutch pedal depressed	(i) Remove foot from clutch pedal to engage clutch as starter works through the clutch
	(ii) Starter lever not returning to normal position for pulling	(ii) Check the spring and replace if weak or broken
	(iii) Starter cable broken	(iii) Replace cable
	(iv) Clutch slipping	(iv) Adjust clutch for correct free movement of the toggle arm
2. Engine will not start (electric starter)	(i) Battery discharged	(i) Check condition of battery e.g. switch on lights and see if dim
	(ii) Disconnected leads	(ii) Check through wiring (see appropriate wiring diagram, Chapter X)
3. Engine turns over only very slowly on starter (electric starter)	(i) Battery low	(i) Check condition of battery
	(ii) Battery faulty	(ii) Battery does not hold charge
	(iii) Starter motor fault	(iii) Brushes may require renewing
4. Engine will not start	(i) No petrol	(i) Check tank and refill, if necessary
	(ii) Petrol in tank but no fuel reaching carburettor— (a) Blockage in feed	(ii) (a) Check if petrol feed pipe is blocked or fractured
	(b) Air lock	(b) Check if air vent in filler cap is blocked
	(c) Blockage in feed	(c) Check if filter in banjo is clogged
	(d) Blockage in carburettor	(d) Check if fuel needle is sticking in seating
	(e) Air lock	(e) Move both main and reserve taps to "on" and fill tank. Check (b) above
	(iii) Engine flooded (too much petrol) (a) Excessive choke	(iii) (a) Close choke control, open throttle wide. (See also Chapter II for details of starting technique.) If badly overchoked it may be necessary to remove and dry the plug
	(b) Use of choke when engine is hot	(b) As for (a)
	(c) Incorrect carburettor adjustment	(c) Re-set taper needle correctly
	(iv) Poor ignition. The usual cause is the plug, viz— (a) Plug dirty	(iv) (a) Clean plug
	(b) Plug gap incorrect	(b) Reset plug electrode gap to 0·018 in.–0·025 in.
	(c) Plug faulty (e.g. insulator cracked or damp)	(c) Dry plug if insulator is definitely wet. Otherwise replace plug
	(d) Incorrect type of plug	(d) Replace with correct type, viz—Lodge H.H.14
	(e) Disconnexion	(e) Check ignition lead
	(f) Lead earthing	(f) Check condition of all leads on ignition circuit

Trouble or Symptom(s)	Possible cause	Remedy
4. Engine will not start—(contd.)	(g) Faulty ignition coil or condenser (if traced to the magneto unit, a contact-breaker fault is most probable—so check this first)	(g) The generator may be checked for spark: remove plug and detach lead; hold lead about $\tfrac{3}{16}$ in. from cylinder and turn engine over; a good spark should jump the gap between the end of the lead and the cylinder. If no spark is generated at the end of the ignition lead, check the wiring
	(h) Faulty ignition switch	(h) Prove fault by removing appropriate wires before replacing
	(i) Contact-breaker gap incorrect	(i) Readjust points to 0·015 in. gap
	(j) Contact-breaker points dirty or pitted	(j) Clean points or reface, as necessary. Adjust to 0·015 in. gap
	(k) Contact breaker faulty	(k) Check for cracked insulation or cable fault
	(l) High tension lead pick-up (in magneto) insulated	(l) Check if incorrectly positioned. Clean if necessary
	(m) Mixture too lean	(m) Choke not operated
	(n) Air leaks on fuel supply system	(n) Check for loose connexions on carburettor
5. Engine starts but stops again after a short run	(i) Lack of fuel	(i) Petrol tap may not be turned on, or tank is empty
	(ii) Mixture too lean	(ii) If weather is cold, leave choke operated for a little longer
	(iii) Spark plug lead disconnected by vibration	(iii) Check and replace
6. Engine runs badly (idling and moderate speeds)	(i) Incorrect mixture—too rich: generally characterized by an excessively smoky exhaust	(i) (a) Make sure choke is open ("off") (b) Carburettor may require adjustment or cleaning (c) Carburettor fuel needle may be sticking or float punctured
	(ii) Incorrect mixture—too lean	(ii) (a) Check for possible air leaks (b) Carburettor may require adjustment
7. Engine lacks power or does not run well at high speeds	(i) Air leak causing loss of compression	(i) Check and tighten cylinder head if loose
	(ii) Contact-breaker fault	(ii) *See* Chapter X
	(iii) Wrong fuel	(iii) Check petrol-oil mixture
	(iv) Wrong plug	(iv) Plug too "hot" or too "cold"; check by appearance and replace, if necessary
	(v) Worn engine	(v) Loss of compression through worn piston rings and bore
	(vi) Worn bearings	(vi) Requires major overhaul
	(vii) Exhaust system partially blocked with carbon	(vii) Decarbonize exhaust and silencer

FAULT FINDING

Trouble or Symptom(s)	Possible cause	Remedy
7. Engine lacks power or does not run well at high speeds —(contd.)	(viii) Engine choked with carbon	(viii) Decarbonize engine *Note:* (vii) will occur before (viii). When decarbonizing the exhaust is no longer effective, then the engine requires decarbonizing (see Chapter V, Sect. 12)
	(ix) Ignition timing incorrect	(ix) Spark timing should be checked and readjusted, if necessary
	(x) Excess load— (a) Final drive chain too tight (b) Brakes binding	(x) (a) Check and readjust chain tension (b) Adjust properly (a check is to see if the car will roll easily when pushed with the handbrake off and engine stopped in neutral)
	(xi) Fuel mixture incorrect	(xi) See Chapter II
8. Engine will not "idle" properly (*Note:* a single-cylinder two-stroke engine cannot be expected to idle as smoothly as a car engine and a certain amount of roughness in running is inevitable)	(i) Mixture wrong (ii) Crankcase leak (iii) Worn engine (iv) Worn bearings (v) Ignition fault	(i) *See carburettor details in Chapters VI and VIII* (ii) Check if drain plug is missing or loose (iii) Overhaul required (iv) Overhaul required (v) *See Chapters X and XI*
9. Engine stops suddenly after a long run	(i) No spark— (a) Plug lead (b) Plug (c) High tension lead earthed	(i) (a) Plug lead replaced (b) Clean plug (c) Plug may have become wet with water, shorting the high tension supply to earth: dry out
	(ii) Engine seized	(ii) Could be caused by running on incorrect mixture—e.g. too little or no oil; and by lack of oil in engine crankcase or gearbox
10. No lights	(i) Battery dead	(i) Check and look for cause e.g. shorting wire
	(ii) Light switch faulty Wiring fault	(ii) If check of battery and bulbs independently shows these components satisfactory, look for fault in circuit
11. Lights dim	(i) Battery low	(i) Should pick up with engine running; if not, then (ii)
	(ii) Faulty generator or rectifier	(ii) Get generator circuit checked by service station
	(iii) Wrong bulbs	(iii) Check bulb sizes against specification
12. Fuse blows	(i) Battery connected wrong way round	(i) Check that *positive* terminal of battery is connected to earth
	(ii) Wrong fuse rating	(ii) Replace with standard 15-amp fuse
	(iii) Wiring fault	(iii) Look for frayed insulation, bared lead ends touching metal bodywork, etc.

DYNASTART ELECTRICAL UNITS

Trouble or Symptom(s)	Possible cause	Remedy

1. Starter does not operate when ignition key is turned*	(i) Battery low
	(ii) Poor connexions
	(iii) Wiring fault
	(iv) Solenoid fault
	(v) Starter fault—
	  (a) Armature fouling stator
	  (b) Brush faulty
	  (c) Oil on commutator
	  (d) Electrical fault
		(i) Check battery acid level
		(ii) Clean battery terminals and lead ends
		(iii) Check wiring
		(iv) Check switch and connexions
		(v) (a) Check by hand rotation
		  (b) Check if brushes worn or sticking
		  (c) Clean, but check also source of oil
		  (d) Replacement unit will probably be required

2. Starter spins engine but engine does not start	(i) Ignition fault—
	  (a) Plug
	  (b) Contact breaker
	  (c) Contact breaker stiff
	  (d) Condenser fault
	  (e) Ignition coil fault
	  (f) Wiring fault
		(i) (a) Plug dirty or wrong gap
		  (b) Check gap and readjust. Clean points
		  (c) Clean and grease pin
		  (d) Replace condenser
		  (e) Replace coil
		  (f) Check and rectify

3. Poor running of engine	(i) Ignition fault (ii) Faulty timing cam	(i) Check timing and readjust, if necessary (*otherwise see* Chapter XI) (ii) Replace
4. No ignition warning lamp	(i) Broken bulb (ii) Battery flat (iii) Wiring fault	(i) Replace (ii) Check acid level and charge (iii) Look for disconnected lead and rectify
5. Ignition warning lamp stays alight with engine speeded up†	(i) Wiring fault (ii) Fault in cut-out (iii) Fault in regulator	(i) Check and rectify (ii) Replace switch assembly box (iii) Replace switch assembly box

Note: see **Chapter X**, Figs. 62–65 *for appropriate wiring diagrams.*

* If when it is known that the battery is not discharged the starter fails to turn the engine properly, do not continue to turn the key as serious damage may result. Check for faults first.

† If green light fails to extinguish at "revs" the reversing arrangement may not be operative.

CHAPTER V

DETAILED MAINTENANCE

THE Bond Minicar uses British standard thread sizes throughout. Standard Bond Minicar parts and spares are produced by Sharp's Commercials. All engine spares are standard Villiers production, separately coded and designated. Conversion sets have been produced covering a number of modifications to early models (as detailed in Chapter IX). Parts required should always be related to the engine and chassis number of the vehicle, bearing in mind that an older-type vehicle may already have been modified in some respects (which again can be checked by reference to Chapter IX).

Clutch. The clutch differs appreciably on the earlier (6E and 8E) and later model engines (9E), the former comprising a single-plate and the latter a multi-plate assembly. More complete details on the clutch will be found in the respective chapters dealing specifically with the Villiers engines.

Adjustment of the clutch on the Mark "C" is provided at both ends of the clutch cable, and by the knurled knob protruding from the gearbox casing above the starter arm spindle. Adjustment is normally done by this knurled nut, rotating until the clutch arm at the end has $\frac{1}{8}$ in. free movement, i.e. that amount of free travel before the pressure of the clutch springs begins to be taken up. The nut holds its setting by virtue of the spring clip bearing down against it.

Adjustment of the cable should not normally be necessary, although of course this will be required when a new cable is fitted. It is generally easiest to work on the upper end cable adjuster in this case as the bottom adjuster is more difficult to reach.

On the Mark "D" and Mark "E" and "F" models the adjuster is hidden behind the gearbox cover plate but the end of the knurled nut is fitted with a slotted head screw coming opposite a hole in the casing, *see* Fig. 15. A screwdriver can be inserted through this hole to engage the slot and thus turn the adjuster. The procedure for clutch adjustment is then as follows—

(i) Slacken off the cable adjuster lock nut and screw in the adjuster until slack is obtained in the cable.

(ii) Engage a screwdriver with the adjuster and turn until the end of the clutch lever is 1 in. from the face of the inner casing (*see* Fig. 16).

(iii) Unscrew the cable adjuster until there is $\frac{1}{16}$ in. free movement left on the clutch lever and tighten the adjuster lock nut in this position.

It is possible that no satisfactory adjustment of the clutch can be obtained with either the adjuster screw or the cable adjuster; then the

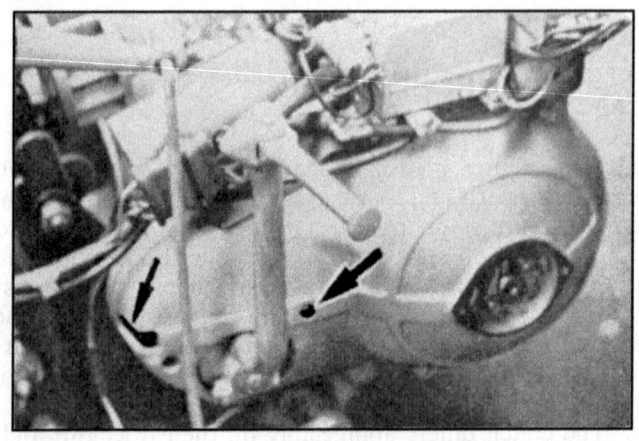

Fig. 15. Adjustment of Clutch (1)

Clutch adjuster is reached through hole in cover plate (arrowed) on 9E engine. Clutch lever position can be seen through slot in rear (arrowed).

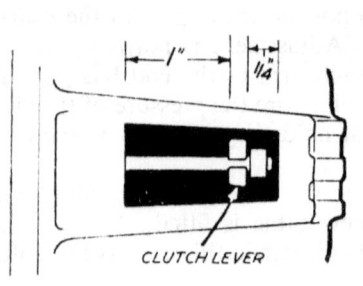 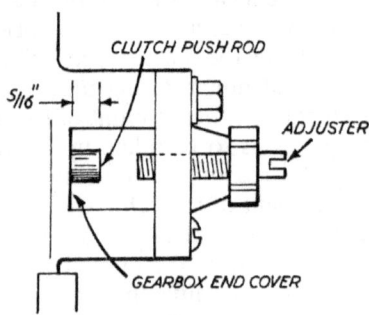

Fig. 16. Adjustment of Clutch (2)

Correct adjustment for clutch is with lever positioned as shown.

Fig. 17. Adjustment of Clutch (3)

Adjustment of clutch push rods is done from chain-case side (chain case cover removed, also the clutch lever, to measure exact protrusion of end rod).

adjustment will have to be made by resetting the clutch push rods. One push rod protrudes from the gearbox end cover on the chain-case side (under the cover), (*see* Fig. 17), the correct amount of protrusion being $\frac{5}{16}$ in. This can be set by turning the adjusting screw in the centre of the clutch cap nut and tightening up the lock nut to hold this setting (*see also* Chapter VI *and* Chapter VIII *for clutch details*).

On all Mark "G" models clutch adjustment is provided at the pedal end of the clutch cable and also by a slotted adjuster on the gearbox end cover. Slackening the cable adjuster lock nut at the pedal end enables the adjuster to be screwed in until slack is obtained in the cable. At the gearbox cover end then slacken the lock nut on the slotted end adjuster screw and turn this screw with a screwdriver until a measurement of $2\frac{1}{4}$ in. is obtained between the outside face of the end of the clutch lever and the outside face of the gearbox end cover. This measurement should be taken with the end of the clutch lever held in line with the clutch cable and pointing towards the clutch cable guide.

The pedal end adjuster should then be turned until there is $\frac{1}{8}$ in. free movement on the end of the clutch lever (i.e. before resistance of the clutch push rods is felt). Then tighten both lock nuts and finally check that the same $\frac{1}{8}$ in. free movement is available.

If satisfactory adjustment cannot be obtained, this indicates that the clutch push rods need adjustment. Slacken the clutch cable from the pedal end, as above, remove nut and slotted countersunk screw holding the bridge piece in position, followed by the clutch lever, and replace the bridge piece temporarily. Drain oil from the primary chain-case and remove the outer cover. Release the lock nut on the adjuster screw in the end of the clutch cap and turn this screw until a spacing of $\frac{1}{2}$ in. is obtained between the face of the slot on the clutch push rod thrust pad and the underside of the bridge piece. Tighten the lock nut and check that this setting has not shifted. Finally refit clutch lever (replace cover and refill with oil) and adjust the clutch cable as described above.

Brakes. The basic braking system as adopted on all later models is detailed in Fig. 18. The Mark "E" and Mark "F" retain essentially the same layout except that the cross shaft is shorter. The rear brakes are rod-operated throughout on this system (except for the handbrake) and the front brake is cable-operated. Mark "A" and Mark "B" models had no front brake, and the foot pedal system shown was not adopted until 1955 (later Mark "C" models).

The cross shaft is connected to a floor-mounted intermediate lever by a tubular push rod, the front brake cable being taken off this intermediate lever forwards and a central brake rod aft to a transfer lever in the centre of the rear axle channel. Separate push rods connect the transfer lever to each bellcrank lever on the rear trailing arms.

The adjustment on the push rod between the cross shaft and the intermediate lever is purely for initial setting-up and *should not be used for normal brake adjustment*, otherwise the transfer lever will be thrown out of correct alignment. Adjustment of the brakes to compensate for wear is done simply by means of the adjusters, positioned on the short rods between the bellcrank lever and brake drop arm on each rear unit; for the front brake an adjuster is provided at each end of the outer brake cable.

An additional brake adjustment point is provided on each rear brake shoe, intended to be used only when normal adjustment has brought the drop arm past the vertical position (leaning forward) with the brakes fully on. This entails the fitting of packing washers behind the detachable

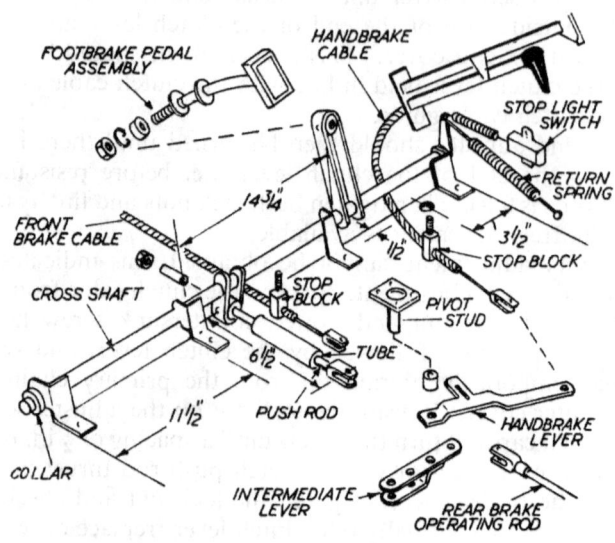

FIG. 18. ARRANGEMENT OF BRAKING SYSTEM

Installation drawn is appropriate to later Mark "C" but remains basically the same on later models. On the Mark "E" and "F" the cross shaft is appreciably shorter.

steel brake shoe pads, when it will be necessary to re-set the brake system since the hubs and brake shoes have to be removed for this operation.

Removal of a rear wheel and hub for the purpose of fitting new brake linings (or carrying out the operation above) requires that the car should be suitably supported (*see* Fig. 19). The road wheel and hub cap are then taken off the hub. Slacken the brake adjustment right off. Take out the split pin securing the castellated nut at the end of the rear axle spindle (offside) and straighten the lock washer on the nearside spindle. Then the nuts can be removed. The hub should then be removed from the spindle by the edge of the brake drum from behind with a block of *wood*.

The front hub is removed by raising and supporting the front of the car, taking off the front wheel and detaching the chain by removing the split link. Remove the hub cap, split pin and castellated nut, slacken off the brake adjustment and knock off the hub, as above. The brake shoe assembly will now be fully exposed.

The shoes can be removed by gripping firmly near the top and lifting clear of the anchor pin, with the springs still attached to the shoes. The springs can then be detached and fitted to the replacement shoes, or to the old shoes after removing the old linings and fitting new.

Before refitting, smear grease (preferably graphited grease) on the anchor pin and camshaft. The assembled shoes are then placed on the cam shaft

Fig. 19. Wheel Removal

Special jack is produced (1959) for the Minicar. However, the vehicle is light enough to be lifted by hand on to a suitable support for removing a wheel, etc. Hub cap (arrowed) is grease-packed.

and prised open to fit on the anchor pin. Check that the springs are adequately anchored around the centre rib of the brake shoes, dust the brake drum clean and tap the hub back in position. The remainder of the assembly then follows as the reverse of the dismantling described above, completing the job by adjusting the brakes individually with the adjuster screw (or cable adjuster in the case of the front brake).

The procedure for resetting the brakes, should the system have been dismantled or otherwise upset at some time, is a little more complicated. The car should be supported clear of the ground (in the case of Mark "E" and Mark "F" models, well inboard from the front and rear bumpers), so that there is easy access to the braking system. Standard procedure, as specified by Sharp's Commercials Ltd., is then as follows—

(i) Set the handbrake to the fully "off" position.

(ii) Release the lock nut on the handbrake cable adjuster and screw the adjuster into the block until the inner cable is slack and the lever to which the cable is attached can be moved freely *or* unscrew the handbrake rod lock nut and adjusters and the master adjuster clear of their respective levers on the cross shaft (*Mark "C" models*).

(iii) Release the adjuster lock nuts on the front-brake cable and screw adjusters into the stop blocks until the inner cable is slack.

(iv) Lift the footbrake pedal until the arm is in contact with the underside of the well, i.e. full off *or* strikes the pedal bracket (*Mark "C"*). Then—

Mark "C" Models

(v) Adjust the push rod between the cross shaft and the brake pedal to give a measurement of $10\frac{3}{4}$ in. between the centres of the trunnions.

(vi) Screw the independent brake-adjustment nuts equally up on the brake rods, allowing approximately $\frac{5}{16}$ in. of thread to protrude to receive the lock nut.

(vii) Adjust the master-adjuster nut on the cross shaft until the brake shoes are binding hard on the brake drums. Then unscrew sufficiently for the wheels to be revolved freely.

(viii) Adjust the handbrake lever for a free pull of two to three notches.

Mark "D," "E" and "F" Models

(v) Adjust the push rod between the cross shaft and intermediate lever to give a measurement of $6\frac{1}{2}$ in. between the centre of the trunnion and the centre of the clevis pin on the intermediate lever.

(vi) Screw the independent brake adjusting nuts equally on the rear units and unscrew the front cable adjusters until all brakes are binding hard. Then readjust until the wheels can be revolved freely.

(vii) Replace the rear-brake rod pull-off springs.

(viii) Adjust the handbrake cable so that the end of the slot in the connecting lever is set approximately $\frac{1}{4}$ in. from contact with the intermediate lever clevis pin.

Mark "G" Models

The Mark "G" models are fitted with a Lockheed braking system with hydraulically operated brake shoes at the front and mechanically operated shoes at the rear, operated by depression of the foot brake pedal. The handbrake operates directly on the mechanical linkage to the rear wheels.

For brake adjustment the whole vehicle should preferably be raised from the ground and suitably supported, although front or rear brake adjustment can be done by raising the end concerned to clear the wheel or wheels from the ground.

Front brake adjustment is carried out by a squared adjuster on the backplate, which should be turned clockwise to bring the shoes into closer contact with the drum. The adjuster should be turned until the shoes bear hard against the drum so that the wheel cannot be turned and then backed off the *minimum* amount necessary for the wheel to revolve freely.

The amount of backing off called for should not normally be more than one or two clicks of the adjuster.

To adjust the back brakes, both rear wheels should be removed and the handbrake put in the "off" position. The notched adjuster is inside the brake and access to it is gained by rotating the drum until the adjuster is exposed by the hole in the drum. Turn the adjuster clockwise until both shoes bear hard against the drum, then turn it back one click at a time, depressing the brake pedal after each click, until the wheel is free. It is important that rear brake adjustment be made *only* with the adjusters. Adjustment of the handbrake cable should never be done to "take up" the brakes. Adjustment of the shoes will automatically adjust the handbrake movement.

If any part of the hydraulic system is disconnected it is essential that the system be "bled" when reassembled and refilled with fluid. One bleed nipple is provided on the front brake backplate and one on the hydraulic frame cylinder. The process of "bleeding" consists in fitting to the bleed nipple a length of rubber tubing dipping into a jar of hydraulic fluid, unscrewing the nipple one complete turn and then repeatedly applying the brake pedal slowly until the fluid flowing from the rubber tube is completely free from traces of air bubbles. When this is so, the brake pedal should be held down and the nipple retightened. Bleeding should be done at the front backplate first, then at the frame cylinder. It is important when "bleeding" to ensure that the level of fluid in the master cylinder is not allowed to fall too low as otherwise air may be drawn into the system, nullifying the effect of "bleeding." Should this occur, then the system would have to be re-bled to clear.

Gearbox (Fig. 20 and Chapter VIII). The gearbox is fully detailed in the chapter covering the Villiers 9E engine, where both the three-speed and four-speed boxes are shown. No internal adjustment of the gearbox is required under normal maintenance and where attention is required by the gearbox this constitutes a major engine overhaul.

Slack which may develop in the gear-change linkage will most probably be due to play developing in the rubber bushes in the rear end of the swivel arm. This can be taken up, slackening the lock nut at the bottom end of the rod which passes down the centre of the steering head spindle, and tightening the pressure nut (securing this again with the lock nut). At the same time, if considerable play has been taken up, this may alter the relative position of the drop arm to the steering-head spindle so that the rod length will require readjustment to prevent fouling.

Transmission. The main chain is fully exposed by removing the chain cover on the left-hand side of the engine. The chain can be detached by removing the spring link. When refitting, the spring link must be replaced *with the closed end facing the direction of travel* of the chain.

Adjustment of the chain is an important feature of routine maintenance since incorrect adjustment will both cause chain wear and possibly affect the operation of the torque reaction linkage resulting in excessive engine vibration. Adjustment procedure differs with the various models. An over-tight chain is probably more damaging than a slack chain, a sag of ⅜ in. being a correct adjustment, measured at the middle of the bottom run.

MARK "A." The front wheel is mounted on an eccentric spindle, the spindle position being adjustable by slackening off the lock nut and

FIG. 20. GEARBOX LINKAGE ON 9E ENGINE WITH DYNASTART UNIT
The standard foot starter is retained for emergency use.
1. Gear-change crank   2. Gear-change linkage   3. Foot starter

inserting a spanner on the square end. The front of the engine must be jacked up or suitably supported with the wheel clear of the ground when making this adjustment. The chain should be tightened until there is approximately ⅜ in. free movement up and down in the middle of its length. Then tighten the lock nut, taking care not to disturb the adjustment.

MARK "B." As for Mark "A."

MARK "C." Adjustment is provided by movement of the engine plates with respect to the fixed shackle plates. The procedure is—

(i) The car must be standing normally on its wheels.

(ii) Release the ½-in. nut holding the engine attachment to the top bolt of the shackle plate.

(iii) Slacken off the nuts on each side of the rear engine and gearbox-mounting bolt.

(iv) Release adjuster lock nut and lift, or block up, the front of the engine slightly to hold the comparative lengths of the torque reaction springs unaltered (alternatively fit a clamp to hold these spring settings).

DETAILED MAINTENANCE

(v) Unscrew the adjuster from the long nut on the rear of the gearbox to move the engine forward, in order to tension the chain for $\frac{3}{8}$ in. sag.

(vi) Tighten the nuts on the engine bolt, the nut on the top shackle bolt and the adjusting screw lock nut.

(vii) Remove the top clamp, or release the engine support, as appropriate.

Mark "D"

(i) As for Mark "C."

(ii) Slacken the bolt securing the silencer unit to its mounting bracket so that it is free to re-position itself when the engine is moved.

(iii) Release the bolt passing through the engine plates and spacing tube (just at the rear of the air filter).

(iv) Unscrew (until free) the bolt through the engine plates and spacer tube, below the bottom of the crankcase.

(v) Pull the engine forward to establish the correct chain tension, as before.

(vi) Tighten up all bolts without disturbing the adjustment.

On all models from the "D" onwards the engine should be moved forwards by hand to give correct chain adjustment. The screw is merely used as a stop, being adjusted with the head against the rear of the engine plate when correct adjustment has been obtained.

Mark "G"

Correct chain adjustment is a $\frac{1}{2}$ in. "lift" or slack when the chain is pressed upwards by the fingers midway between the sprockets. The weight of the car must be on all wheels and the handbrake off when adjusting the chain. To enable the engine to be tilted forwards for adjustment, slacken the silencer clamp bolt and bracket nut and release the two $\frac{3}{8}$ in. set screws passing through the engine plates at the rear of the air cleaner; then slightly unscrew the $\frac{7}{16}$ in. nut from the bolt passing through the engine plates and spacing tube underneath the crankcase.

Carburettor (Figs. 21 and 22, *see also* Fig. 41). Carburettors fitted to the various models are—

    Villiers 6E engine—Villiers Type 4/5
    Villiers 8E engine—Villiers Type S.24 (Mark "C")
                        Villiers Type S.25 (late Mark "C")
    Villiers 9E engine—Villiers Type S.25 (Marks "D" and "E")
    Villiers 31A engine—Villiers Type S.25 (Mark "F")
    Villiers 35A engine—Villiers Type S.25/8 (Mark "G" single-cylinder engine)
    Villiers 4T engine—Villiers Type S.25/11 (Mark "G" twin-cylinder engine)

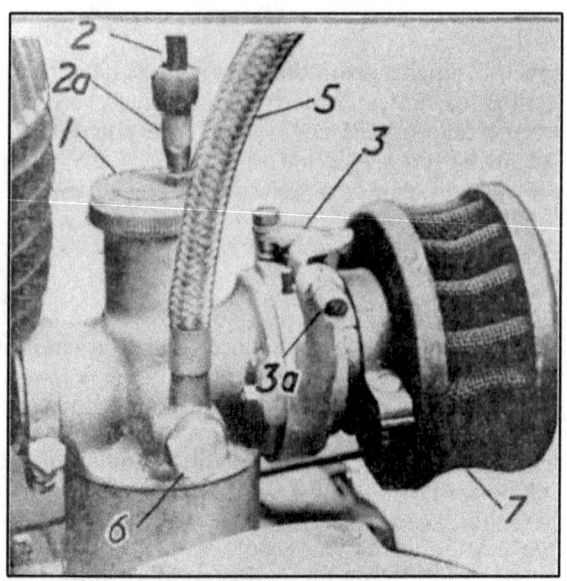

FIG. 21. CARBURETTOR (NEARSIDE VIEW)

1. Top disc
2. Throttle cable
2a. Cable adjuster
3. Choke control (cable not fitted)
3a. Adjuster
5. Fuel pipe
6. Fuel pipe banjo
7. Air filter

FIG. 22. CARBURETTOR (OFFSIDE VIEW)

2. Throttle cable   3. Choke control (cable not fitted)   4. Tickler   5. Fuel pipe

DETAILED MAINTENANCE

Full details of these are included in the chapters on the Villiers engine.

A distinguishing feature between the S.24 and S.25 carburettors is that in the former model the slide is of brass instead of alloy; also the top disc of the S.25 unit is plain and domed. The S.25 carburettor was fitted to Mark "C" models subsequent to Chassis No. F/10/7693. A further improvement in fuel consumption with this engine was produced by setting the taper needle to a length of 2·03 in. instead of the original manufacturer's recommendation of 1·95 in.

FIG. 23. STANDARD PATTERN DECOMPRESSOR
Volumetric type (Easistart compressor) fitted later—recommended for all manual-start models and where self-starter fitted on top of engine engaging via belt drive.

Decompressor (Fig. 23). The only attention this unit should require is an occasional drop of oil on the valve spindle, and periodic regrinding of the valve. The decompressor can be dismantled by unscrewing the valve stem nut, removing the spring and withdrawing the valve. The valve may easily be reseated by coating with abrasive paste, relocating against its seat and grinding in with a rotary motion (e.g. turning the valve head with a screwdriver). This will only be necessary when the valve or seating shows marked signs of pitting or burning.

All traces of abrasive paste should be washed off with petrol before reassembling the valve, and the stem cleaned of carbon and lightly oiled.

Ignition. The wiring systems are fully detailed in Chapter X, and SIBA electrics are fitted to Marks "D," "E" and "F" models as in Chapter XI. Mechanical details of the magneto-generator units fitted to earlier models will also be found in Chapters VII and VIII.

The sparking plug specified for all the Villiers engines is a Lodge HH14 with a recommended gap setting of 0·018 in.—0·025 in. The plug insulator should always be kept clean as oil or dirt on it makes for a weak spark and difficult starting. However, the merits of continuing to use an old plug, although cleaned, almost indefinitely are debatable. The plug is one of the hardest working components of a two-stroke engine and the fitting of a new plug at regular intervals (say every 5,000 miles) is generally good practice. The fact that plugs do readily get fouled up in two-stroke engines makes it essential to carry a reliable spare or new plug adjusted ready for fitting. The spark plug is the source of nearly all ignition faults.

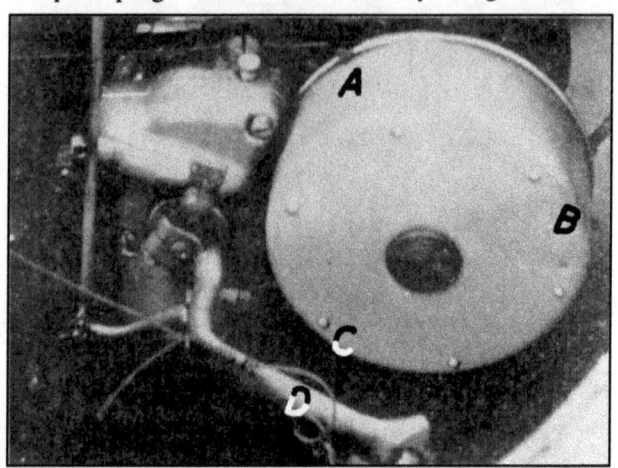

FIG. 24. CONTACT-BREAKER ON THE 6E AND 8E ENGINE
Reached by removing flywheel cover held by three spring clips (*A*, *B*, *C*). Pull the starter arm (*D*) back to clear.

An incorrect fuel mixture, or the wrong type of plug, can result in poor running; the plug being either too "hot" or too "cold" for the mixture which it has to ignite. These terms are used synonymously with "soft" or "hard," respectively. If the plug is too "soft" the points will tend to become corroded with a white deposit and the whole of the inside of the plug will have a whitish-grey appearance. A plug which is too "hard," by comparison, will appear covered with a dense black deposit over the points and the insulator body inside the plug. A correctly-matched plug is one which maintains itself at the correct temperature, for any particular mixture in a standard engine, without formation of deposits or excessive discoloration.

The contact-breaker unit is located in the flywheel magneto. On models up to Mark "C" it is exposed by removing the flywheel cover and turning the flywheel as necessary to gain access; where a self-starter motor is fitted the loose pulley must be removed first (*see* Fig. 24). On later models the contact-breaker is exposed by removing the small cover plate on the right-hand side of the engine crankcase unit (*see* Fig. 38).

Adjustment of the points on the 8E engine can be made by slackening the screw holding the fixed point bracket, and then turning the cam adjuster to arrive at the correct setting of 0·015 in. fully open, *see* Fig. 31. This adjustment is made after first turning the flywheel to raise the rocker arm so that the points are fully opened. On the 9E engine adjustment is similar, but there is no adjusting cam and the point bracket itself is moved to effect the adjustment required. Details of the SIBA unit contact-breakers will be found in Chapter XI. Details of ignition-timing adjustment are given in the engine chapters.

Steering. The early Mark "A" models were fitted with bobbin-and-cable steering, adjustment for tensioning the steering cable being provided by a screw fitting in the cable. The correct tension is that which gives minimum tension with all backlash eliminated.

Later Mark "A" and Mark "B" models feature rack-and-pinion steering. Adjustment, to take up slack, consists simply of slackening off the clamping bolt passing through the top shackle and bracket, tapping down the bracket and retightening the bolt.

If a check shows that there is no appreciable slack or wear in the steering gear, but a definite rattle is heard when running, this is probably due to harmonic vibration; i.e. at a certain engine r.p.m. the vibration of the engine corresponds to the harmonic frequency of the steering unit and so it vibrates in sympathy. It has been found that this apparent fault can be cured completely by dismantling the steering box, washing out all old grease with petrol or paraffin and repacking with "Marfak" Grease No. 6. This grease, incidentally, cannot be dispensed through a grease gun but once the box is packed it should be good for 5,000 miles running, when it can be repacked. The normal 500-mile attention to the steering head is therefore unnecessary.

All later models have worm-and-sector steering. Adjustment is similar on all models.

To take up slack in the steering-head spindle the cotter pin connecting the arm of the gear-change lever to the control rod is withdrawn and the arm swung out of the way. The top lock nut on the steering-head spindle should then be slackened off and a special box spanner dropped over this nut to engage the adjusting nut beneath (*see* Fig. 25). Turn the wheel to half right lock and slacken off the clamp screw. Then the adjusting nut is tightened to take up all the end play, the lock nut retightened, and the gear-change cotter pin replaced.

Provision is made for adjusting the depth of engagement of the worm with the sector gear by slackening off the worm housing and slewing the worm into deeper engagement. The worm and sector gear should never be tightly engaged, however, as this will produce stiff movement and heavy wear on the teeth. This method of adjusting can readily be applied to take up excessive slack in the steering wheel movement.

Up and down slack in the steering-wheel shaft can be taken up by slackening off the lock nut at the end of the worm housing and then turning the adjusting screw with a C-spanner to take up the play, locking the lock nut again in the new position.

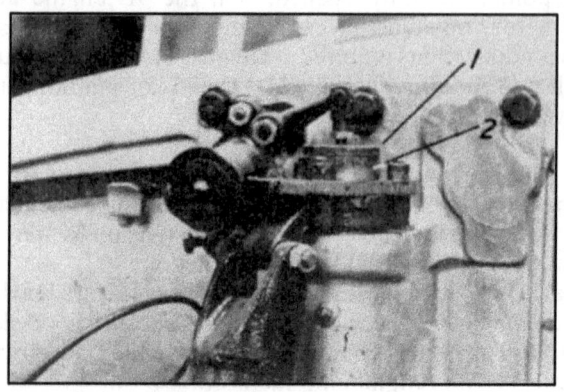

FIG. 25. STEERING-HEAD ADJUSTMENT

To take up play, adjustment is done by slackening locking nut (1) and tightening (2) with a special box spanner. Gear-change lever must be temporarily disconnected.

Rear Suspension (Fig. 26). Bonded-rubber rear suspension was introduced with the Mark "C" model utilizing Flexitor units, which units have subsequently been fitted to all later models (in an improved form on later models). No maintenance or lubrication is necessary, or possible (*see* Chapter IX *for conversion of earlier models to this form of rear suspension*).

Wheels and Tyres. Except in the case of the original Mark "A" Minicar, wheel removal simply involves unscrewing the six *inner* (cap) nuts and washers and lifting the wheel off its studs (*see* Fig. 27). The appropriate side or end of the car will, of course, need to be jacked-up or suitably supported to do this. Although a special jack for the Minicar was introduced in 1959, the weight of the car is such that it is readily possible simply to lift the front or rear end on to a suitable support.

In the case of the Mark "A," the tyre must first be deflated before removing the wheel since the same six nuts also hold the split rims together and, if undone with the tyre inflated, would burst apart with some violence. On later models (Mark "C" onwards) the rims are separated to remove the tyre by undoing the outer ring of nuts, again *not attempting this before the tyre is completely deflated.*

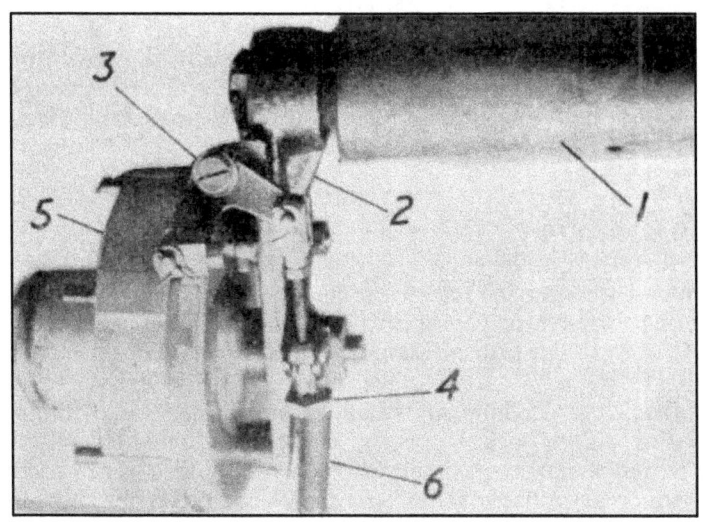

Fig. 26. Latest "Flexitor" Unit detached from Vehicle
The bracket bolts to underside of floor.

1. Fixing bracket
2. Trailing arm
3. Brake link (bellcrank)
4. Brake adjuster
5. Wheel hub
6. Return spring

Fig. 27. Rear Wheel

Unscrew the six cap nuts (1) to remove wheel. Nuts (2) separate rims, but tyre must first be completely deflated. Inflation point at (3).

Recommended tyre pressures are summarized in the table in Chapter III; it is important to keep tyres as near as possible to recommended pressures both for maximum ride comfort and maximum tyre life. It will also pay to change the wheels around every 3,000 miles or so to equalize the wear.

Speedometer Drive. The speedometer on the Mark "A" model is driven directly from the engine gearbox via a belt. On all other models it is driven off the nearside rear-wheel hub, a spindle bolted to the hub cap protruding through the centre of the axle shaft and engaging the flexible cable drive to the instrument mounted on the facia panel.

Decarbonizing. Definite signs that an engine needs decarbonizing are overheating and/or lack of power, particularly a reluctance to "pull" properly under maximum acceleration, or under load (as in ascending a hill in top gear). These same symptoms can, of course, be caused by incorrect ignition timing which would be the first thing to suspect if the engine has recently been decarbonized (within the last 2–3,000 miles).

Initially the main deposit of carbon will be in the silencer and exhaust port, which can be dealt with simply by detaching the silencer complete, cleaning out the exhaust port and dismantling the silencer for cleaning. The silencer is first detached from the exhaust pipe and, if the nut is removed from the end of the tailpipe, the centre section can be withdrawn from the silencer body (straight-through type silencer).

The complete engine can, however, be decarbonized without removing the engine from the frame. Disconnect the high-tension lead and remove the plug. Detach the decompressor cable and unscrew the decompressor. The four cylinder-head bolts (Fig. 28) are then unscrewed allowing the cylinder head to be lifted off.

The flexible fuel pipe is then detached from the carburettor (making sure that the fuel tap is switched off), and the carburettor and air filter with manifold are removed by unscrewing the set screws on the inlet manifold flange.

The silencer unit is removed complete, releasing the exhaust pipe locking ring with a C-spanner and unscrewing the silencer-supporting bolt.

The cylinder barrel can then be released by unscrewing the four nuts at the base, having previously turned the engine to bring the piston to the top of its stroke. Then draw the cylinder barrel off, vertically upwards. Finally remove the piston rings from the piston and the engine is dismantled, ready for decarbonizing. Note: an expander ring may be fitted below the second ring on some engines (e.g. 9E and 31A engines).

All carbon deposits on the top (crown) of the piston and the cylinder head should be scraped off with a piece of wood or a *soft* metal scraper. All the ports in the cylinder barrel should also be cleaned carefully and all the components washed in petrol or clean paraffin. Any gummy or carbon deposits in the piston ring grooves can be cleaned out carefully with a suitable scraper, taking care not to score the soft metal of the piston. Lightly oil the ring grooves before replacing the rings, wipe over the piston with clean oil before starting reassembly, and smear oil over the inside of the cylinder. Check the condition of the gaskets and, if necessary, replace with new. Replace rings, if damaged or worn.

The cylinder barrel can now be slid over the piston, holding the rings compressed, making sure that the cylinder is the correct way round

FIG. 28. CYLINDER HEAD
Four bolts holding cylinder head arrowed. Before removing head first detach high tension lead, decompressor lead and spark plug.

(exhaust port to the front). Avoid rotating the barrel in replacing it as one of the rings may become trapped in a port opening if this is done.

Secure the cylinder block with the four bottom nuts and washers and replace the head with the head gasket between, making sure that the mating surfaces are perfectly clean. The head is positioned with the spark plug hole to the offside. Replace plug, decompressor, cables and carburettor unit (*see* Fig. 29).

Body Repairs. Major body repairs will normally call for professional attention. Minor damage, however, may be attended to by the owner at some considerable saving in cost. Aluminium, as used throughout the body panels and elsewhere, is a relatively soft metal; a dent can often be knocked out by hammering from the underside against a suitable dolly backing the other side and final irregularities filled in with a proprietary resin-base filler such as "Bondafiller."

Cracks in the metalwork, particularly in the stressed-skin body, must first be "isolated" by drilling a hole at the extreme ends of the crack. This will prevent the crack from spreading further. The most satisfactory

Fig. 29. Cable Replacement, etc.

After decarbonizing, check that assembly is correct.

1. Throttle cable   3. Choke cable   5. High tension cable
2. Flexible fuel pipe   4. Decompressor cable

Engine serial number is shown on plate (arrowed).
Engine number must be quoted if spare parts are required.

treatment is then to bolt or rivet a backing plate to the original skin of somewhat greater area than the extent of the crack.

Fibreglass components are used on certain models (*see* Chapter I) and damage to Fibreglass mouldings can be repaired with glass cloth or tape and polyester resin (again there are several proprietary car repair kits of this type on the market). A way of getting a satisfactorily smooth outer surface on a repair is to tape a sheet of cellulose acetate over the area, building up the repair from the inside. Fibreglass repairs can also be applied successfully to damaged metalwork; the resins used have excellent adhesion to aluminium. The main secret of good adhesion is to ensure that the surfaces to which the Fibreglass is to be stuck are clean (completely free from oil, grease or paint) and absolutely dry.

All body paintwork on Minicars is of air-drying cellulose-synthetic type. Colours will generally be difficult to match exactly for touching-up, since the shade of cellulose finishes generally changes with ageing. If applied to bare metal, first treat the metal with an etching-type primer (light alloy type) to ensure good adhesion.

CHAPTER VI

VILLIERS 6E AND 8E ENGINES

THE engine fitted to the original Mark "A" Minicar was the Villiers Mark 10D of 122 c.c. capacity. Very few of these models were produced, however, the 197 c.c. Mark 6E Villiers engine being adopted as standard. Basically this differed only in bore and stroke from the 10D, giving increased capacity and power. The number of teeth on the engine sprocket and clutch sprocket differed, but the same gearbox was used.

The Villiers 8E engine was introduced on the Mark "C" Minicar, after an initial production run with the 6E; it remained standard until the appearance of the Mark "D" Minicar. Broadly speaking the main details

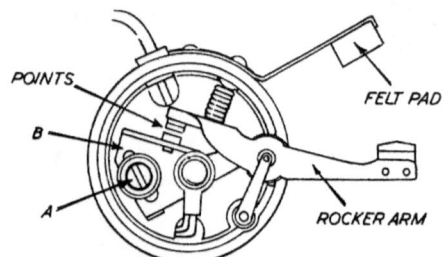

FIG. 30. CONTACT-BREAKER ASSEMBLY ON THE VILLIERS 6E ENGINE
Adjustment is made by loosening *A* and moving point bracket *B*.

of the Villiers 8E engine apply also to the 6E and so only the former is illustrated in detail in this chapter.

The Villiers 6E and 8E engines feature a contact-breaker, readily accessible from the right-hand side of the engine once the flywheel cover is removed. The flywheel cover is merely held on by three spring clips; once these are released it can be pulled off, pushing the starter lever backwards to clear.

In the case of a Mark "A," "B" or "C" model fitted with a self-starter, the loose pulley must be removed by pushing the belt on to the rim of the flywheel and unscrewing the centre nut holding the pulley. With this nut and washer removed the loose pulley can be withdrawn.

Access to the contact-breaker is then gained by rotating the flywheel until a space between the arms comes opposite the contact-breaker unit. The contact-breaker assembly of the 6E engine is drawn in Fig. 30. Screw *A* releases the point bracket *B*, adjustment is made by slackening

A and moving *B* to adjust the gap between the fixed and moving points to 0·015 in., using a feeler gauge between the points. The flywheel must, of course, be turned to the position where the cam on the armature shaft (crankshaft) is lifting the contact-breaker to the fullest extent (i.e. giving maximum "lift" to the moving point).

There will, normally, be no necessity to remove the flywheel (except for dismantling the engine, etc.) but, if this has been done or if the timing requires adjustment, the timing is reset as follows.

(i) Turn the engine over with the starter lever until the piston is at top dead centre.

(ii) Slide the flywheel on to the crankshaft taper.

(iii) Adjust the position of the flywheel until the mark on the armature plate is exactly opposite the mark on the rim of the flywheel. Check that

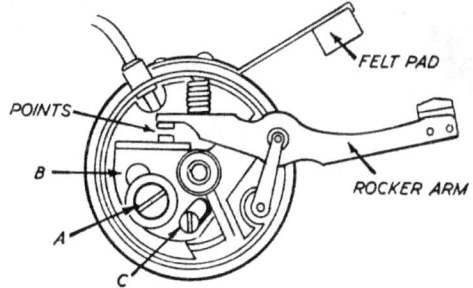

Fig. 31. Contact-breaker Assembly on the Villiers 8E Engine

Adjustment is made by loosening screw *A* and then turning the cam adjuster *C* to position the point bracket *B* correctly.

the piston position has not been disturbed and tighten up the flywheel centre nut. Check piston position again to see that the setting has not been disturbed.

As an additional check the cylinder head can be removed and distance of the piston travel at which the points begin to open can be measured. This should be exactly $\frac{5}{32}$ in. before top dead centre position of the piston.

The contact-breaker assembly on the 8E Villiers engine is shown in Fig. 31. Access is as before but, to facilitate adjustment, a cam screw *C* is provided. The point bracket *B* is first released by slackening off screw *A*; turning screw *C* then adjusts the setting of the point gap. When correct, tighten screw *A* again, taking care not to overtighten and strip the thread.

Very little attention should be required by the contact-breaker unit, except for occasional adjustment of the points gap and, when necessary, cleaning or refacing the points dead flat with a very fine file. The felt pad is grease-impregnated and may eventually require further lubrication. The best plan is to remove it entirely, clean if necessary and re-impregnate with grease by dipping it into molten high-temperature grease, allowing it to cool before replacing. It is not good practice to oil this pad, as excess oil may travel into the contact-breaker unit and get on the points. The

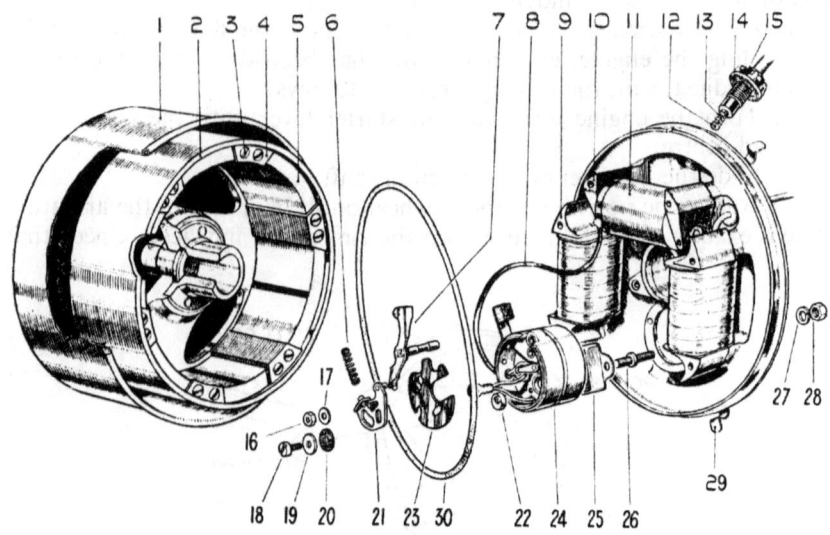

Fig. 32. Flywheel-magneto Assembly on the Villiers 8E Engine

1. Flywheel lever
2. Flywheel
3. Pole-shoe screw
4. Pole shoe
5. Magnet
6. Rocker-arm spring
7. Rocker arm
8. Low tension lead
9. Lighting coils
10. H.T. coil pole piece
11. H.T. coil
12, 13, 14, 15. Terminal assembly
16. L.T. lead nut
21. Point bracket
22. Adjuster cam
23. Insulating pad
24. Condenser box
25. Condenser

(In this and similar illustrations only major items are listed.)

cam may, however, be smeared with a *little* oil from time to time if it seems very dry.

The complete flywheel unit is shown in detail in Fig. 32. Normally a fault on this unit would be referred to a specialist service agent for attention although, of course, the unit will have to be removed during a complete strip-down of the engine (although not necessarily itself completely dismantled).

The carburettor on the Villiers 6E engine is a Villiers type 4/5 with two lever controls. The carburettor fitted to the 8E engine is either a Villiers type S.24 or S.25 (*see* Chapter V, Section 5). The mixture strength

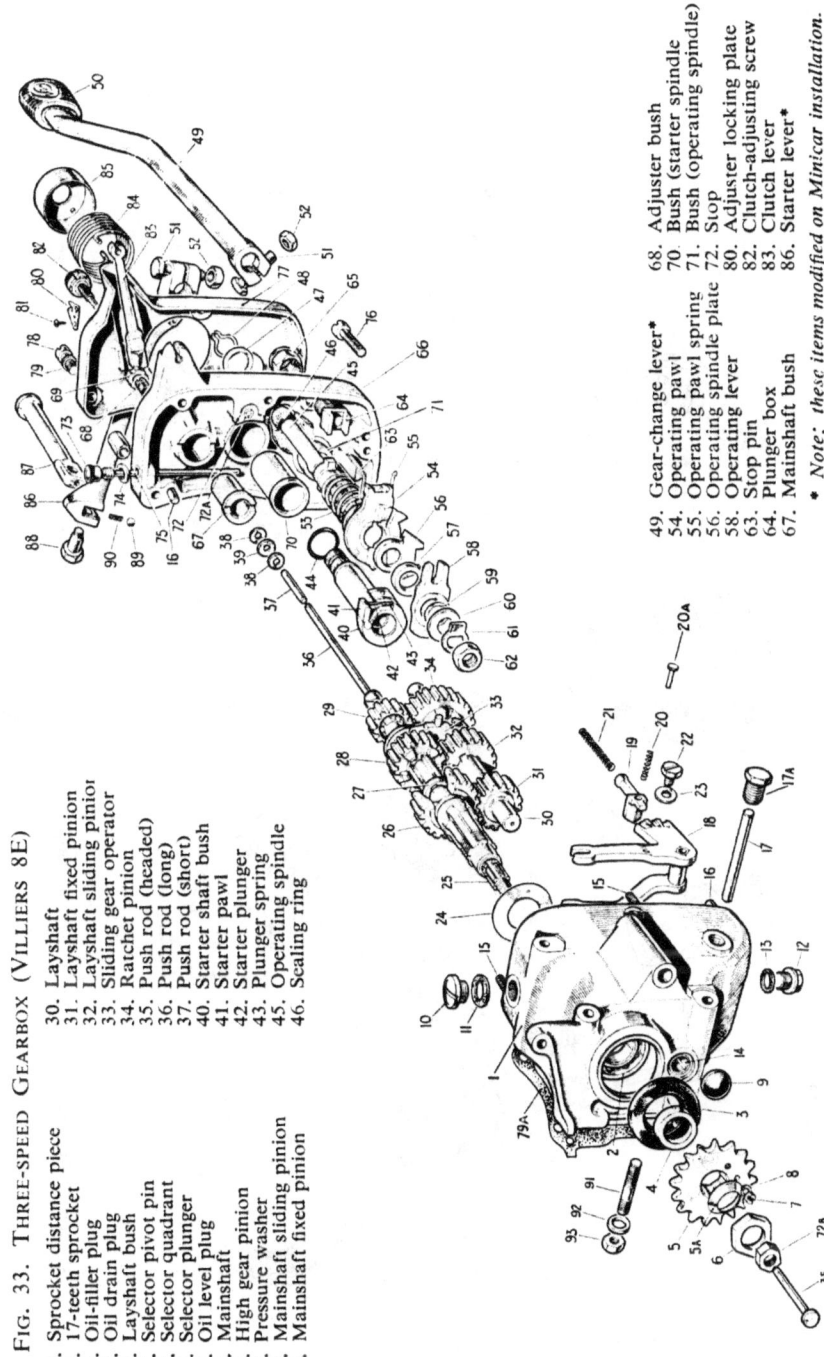

Fig. 33. Three-speed Gearbox (Villiers 8E)

4. Sprocket distance piece
5. 17-teeth sprocket
10. Oil-filler plug
12. Oil drain plug
14. Layshaft bush
17. Selector pivot pin
18. Selector quadrant
19. Selector plunger
22. Oil level plug
25. Mainshaft
26. High gear pinion
27. Pressure washer
28. Mainshaft sliding pinion
29. Mainshaft fixed pinion
30. Layshaft
31. Layshaft fixed pinion
32. Layshaft sliding pinion
33. Sliding gear operator
34. Ratchet pinion
35. Push rod (headed)
36. Push rod (long)
37. Push rod (short)
40. Starter shaft bush
41. Starter pawl
42. Starter plunger
43. Plunger spring
45. Operating spindle
46. Sealing ring
49. Gear-change lever*
54. Operating pawl
55. Operating pawl spring
56. Operating spindle plate
58. Operating lever
63. Stop pin
64. Plunger box
67. Mainshaft bush
68. Adjuster bush
70. Bush (starter spindle)
71. Bush (operating spindle)
72. Stop
80. Adjuster locking plate
82. Clutch-adjusting screw
83. Clutch lever
86. Starter lever*

* Note: these items modified on Minicar installation.

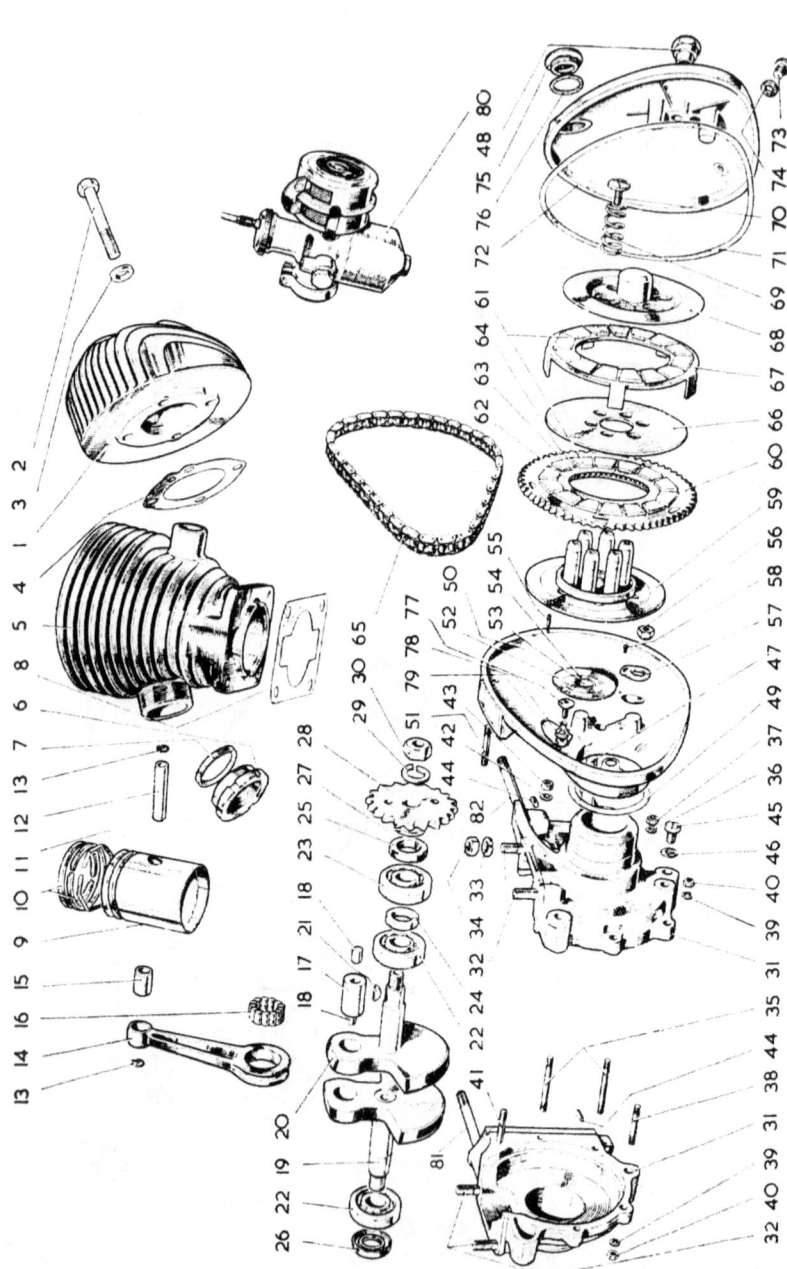

Fig. 34. The Villiers 8E Engine

is determined by the setting of the taper needle, which is adjusted by a screw in the centre at the top of the throttle slide (or in the mixture control cable on the type 4/5 carburettor).

On the Villiers 4/5 carburettor the centre control cable governs the mixture, the other cable governs the accelerator control. The adjuster on the centre cable alters the position of the needle, screwing-in to weaken and screwing-out to enrich. An adjusting nut for setting the idling speed is fitted to the top where the accelerator cable joins the carburettor. Screwing the nut in lowers the engine (idling) speed, unscrewing it speeds the engine up.

On the S.25 type carburettor the centre cable is attached to the slide, whilst the other is a choke cable connecting to a butterfly shutter in the air intake. Both cables are provided with adjusters at the carburettor end. Needle adjustment is by means of the screw in the top of the slide. The slow-running adjustment, on both the S.24 and S.25 units, is provided by a spring-loaded screw in the body of the carburettor.

Normally a carburettor will only require checking or adjusting at infrequent intervals (*see* Chapter III) as the initial settings established by the manufacturers are based on optimum performance. An apparent maladjustment is most likely to be due to some other cause, such as a slight change in petrol-oil proportions, a carburettor leak, blocked air filter, ignition timing fault, etc. If, however, whilst running under load an engine persistently four-strokes, the mixture setting may be weakened slightly to cure it, *see also* Chapter IV *on "fault-finding."* Avoid, however, over-weakening the mixture in an attempt to obtain maximum economy in fuel consumption as this may be damaging to the engine in the long run. In any case, never adjust the needle more than a very small amount at a time.

Slow-running adjustments should always be set when the engine is warm, unscrewing the throttle adjuster until the engine just continues to run without stalling and then adjusting the slow-running screw for smoothest possible running. If this results in too fast an idling speed, the

---

KEY TO FIG 34

2. Cylinder-head bolt
11. Expander ring
12. Gudgeon pin
13. Circlip
14. Connecting rod, bushed, 0·001 in. oversize
15. Small end bush
16. Rollers for crankpin—steel
17. Crankpin
18. Crankpin plug
19. Crankshaft—right-hand
20. Crankshaft—left-hand
21. Key for engine sprocket

28. Engine sprocket
31. Crankcase, right- and left-hand halves, less fittings
44. Dowel in crankcase locating gearbox
50. Chaincase, inner, with gland plate
52. Gland plate
60. Clutch sprocket assembly, comprising items 61–65 inclusive
61. Cork for clutch sprocket and corked plate
62. Ball-retaining plate
65. Primary chain
68. Front-plate assembly

throttle adjustment should be reset and the slow-running screw adjusted again, repeating as necessary until a satisfactory performance is achieved.

When a carburettor is stripped, reassembly can be checked by reference to Fig. 41. The needle valve on the 4/5 carburettor can be changed by unscrewing the top ring and removing the throttle from the body. In the top of the throttle is a small screw which, when removed, allows the needle and spring to be pushed out from underneath. The float chamber can be detached by removing the throttle first and then the bottom nut and fibre washer holding the float chamber in position. The two tubes projecting from the bottom of the throttle chamber must be taken out before the centrepiece can be pushed up from the underside. Follow by swinging the forked lever on the underside of the body to one side, thus allowing the needle to drop out.

Procedure with the S.25 carburettor is similar. The taper needle is removed, as above. To release the fuel needle the main jet screwed to the side of the centrepiece has to be unscrewed in order that the float can be withdrawn, leaving the pilot jet *in situ*.

When reassembling, the centrepiece is inserted first with the forked lever and fuel needle in position. Replace the float (the bottom of which is marked for reference) and the main jet in the side of the body. Replace the float cup (washer uppermost) and the bottom nut and fibre washer, tightening gently. Replace throttle and guide taper needle into hole in centrepiece. Then secure the top with the screw-on ring.

Points to check are that the carburettor is reassembled on the engine in an upright position; that it is pushed on as far as possible so that the manifold does not extend past the ends of the slots and so cause air leaks; and that the clamp screw is properly tightened. The filter in the petrol pipe banjo should be cleaned before refitting the fuel pipe and the fuel pipe properly replaced with the fibre washers to provide a tight seal.

The complete Villiers 8E engine is shown in detail in Figs. 33 and 34.

On the S.25 carburettor the length of the needle is controlled by an adjusting screw; and on the 4/5 carburettor by an adjustment which is located in the centre of the mixture control cable. The recommended settings for each engine are—

E : 2·03 in.   9E : 2·03 in.   31A : 1·95 in.

In the case of the 6E engine which employs the 4/5 carburettor no definite setting can be given. The procedure for setting this carburettor is first to ensure that the engine is warm and then set the throttle adjuster to give a reasonably fast tick-over. Then adjust the mixture control, either richer or weaker, to make the engine speed up, when the throttle control is adjusted again to slow the engine down to a normal tick-over. At this point further adjustment can be made to the mixture control (it will probably require further weakening). Correct setting is a matter of establishing optimum balance between the throttle and mixture controls.

CHAPTER VII

ELECTRIC SELF-STARTER CONVERSION (6E AND 8E ENGINES)

An electric self-starter unit is available as a conversion set for fitting to standard Mark "A," "B" and "C" models, this being quite independent of the manual-starting linkage which can be retained unchanged. Fitting of the self-starter unit follows in this order (applicable to the Mark "C").

First the (manual) starter cable must be disconnected from the starter lever, this lever being withdrawn from the splined shaft by slackening off the clamp bolt. A careful note should be made of the position of this lever so that when replaced it is fitted in its original attitude.

The flywheel cover is then taken off. It is necessary to trim approximately $1\frac{1}{2}$ in. off the edge of this cover so that, when replaced, a $\frac{3}{4}$ in. width of flywheel rim is exposed on which the starter belt can drive. A line for cutting should be scribed round the cover $1\frac{1}{2}$ in. from the wire edge and the cover trimmed to this line with tinsnips. Remove any sharp edges and replace.

The loose pulley is fitted next, tightening the special stud in the end of the flywheel withdrawal nut, putting the pulley on the stud and securing with a nut and washer.

At this stage the engine should be suitably supported from underneath (e.g. rested on a block of wood). Release the engine torque reaction linkage, swivel clear of the cylinder head and then remove the head. The four studs are inserted in the cylinder block face and tightened right up, the coarse threaded ends of these studs fitting the cylinder block. The head can then be refitted using the original washers but new special length nuts. These nuts are tightened progressively in rotation to avoid distortion. The short studs in the top of each cylinder nut are then tightened.

The torque reaction spindle is removed by unscrewing the two nuts from the end. The spindle collar is removed and this collar refitted on the modified spindle $4\frac{3}{4}$ in. from the threaded end, measured to the top side of the collar. Assemble the spindle and springs in the top link with the two nuts, which should come level with the end of the spindle.

The starter motor mounting plate, with starter attached, can now be mounted on the four studs. The torque reaction linkage fits on the rear studs, with a washer under the rear right-hand (offside) stud only, and on the two front studs. Secure with nuts (*see* Fig. 35).

There is a possibility that when the drive is assembled the belt may foul the cheese-head set screw on the top right-hand side of the gearbox endplate and to avoid this the head of the screw can be reduced about $\frac{1}{16}$ in. by filing.

To fit the belt, slacken off the starter-motor bolts and swing the starter to its lowest point. With the belt in place the starter motor position is readjusted to give the correct belt tension, e.g. just enough tension for the starter to turn the engine without the belt slipping along the flywheel or off its rim. The assembly is then complete except for replacement of the manual starter lever and cable. In some cases, however, it may be necessary to crank this lever slightly to clear the bolt in the loose pulley.

FIG. 35. SELF-STARTER UNIT
Mounted on special bracket fitted to cylinder head via special studs.
Belt drive to flywheel via pulley.

The heavy duty battery required with a starter unit is an Exide 6-volt 57 ampere-hour type 3-LH.11L (or equivalent). This battery is too large to carry on a bulkhead or wing mount and so is fitted in the luggage boot at the rear. Place the battery carrier as shown in Fig. 36, scribe the mounting hole positions and drill these through the floor with a $\frac{3}{16}$-in. drill. The carrier is then fixed with countersunk head bolts. A $\frac{1}{4}$-in. drill is used for the two battery bolt holes, drilled at each side of the carrier parallel with the axle channel.

The starter switch is mounted on the underside of the bulkhead panel, approximately $10\frac{3}{4}$ in. from the floor and bulkhead panel joint and 2 in.

ELECTRIC SELF-STARTER CONVERSION

from the outside edge of the panel, in a ⅜-in. diameter hole drilled at this point. The floor of the boot is also drilled with a ¾-in. diameter hole about 1½ in. in front of the battery carrier and the hole fitted with a large

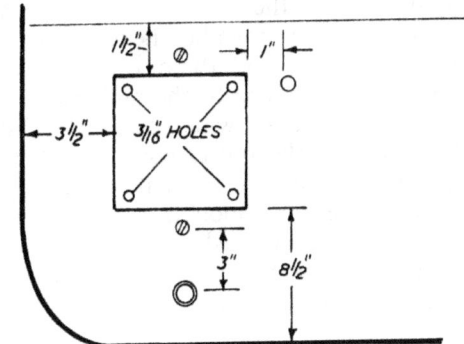

FIG. 36. LOCATION OF BATTERY
Carrier on rear floor of boot to take the new heavy-duty battery.

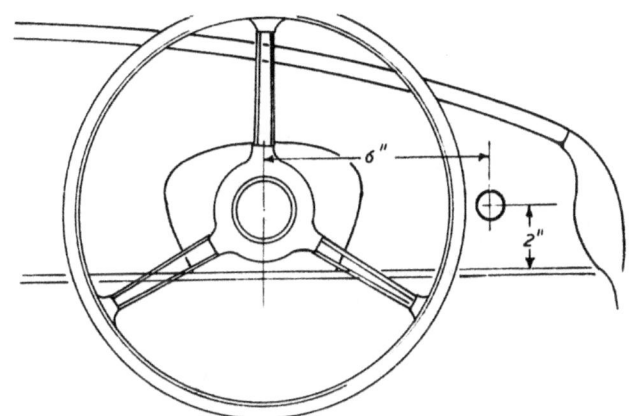

FIG. 37. STANDARD POSITION FOR THE FITTING OF THE STARTER CONTROL ON FACIA
A ⅜-in. diameter hole is required. Similar hole in bulkhead is drilled 2-in. from the outside edge of the panel.

rubber grommet. A ⅜-in. diameter hole is drilled in the facia, as shown in Fig. 37, to fit the starter control housing.

Wiring can be followed by reference to Fig. 60, Chapter X. The spade terminal end of the starter cable is fed through the rubber grommet at the rear, and the cable taken along the underside of the floor to the starter switch in the space between the wing and side panel. Secure with about six evenly-spaced cable clips.

The spade end of the cable is connected to the starter switch terminal nearest the edge of the panel and should be insulated with a rubber sleeve or a generous binding of insulating tape. One end of the remaining length of cable is then connected to the starter motor terminal, position the cable over the suspension spring to the bulkhead panel and finally connect it to the starter switch terminal. Both these connexions are insulated with rubber sleeves. The cable is clipped to the bulkhead, allowing sufficient free length for the engine unit to swing to full lock either side. Final connexions are then made to the starter control switch coupling and to the terminal block and starter switch terminal. (The original battery leads are disconnected from the terminal block.)

The new battery is, of course, charged before being fitted and is mounted with the negative terminal facing forward. Bolt the *positive* earth strap to the floor, making sure of a good metal-to-metal contact.

CHAPTER VIII

THE VILLIERS 9E AND 250 C.C. ENGINE

THE Villiers 9E engine is standard on the Mark "D and Mark "E" Minicar, the various models employed being—

Mark 9E/3	3-speed gearbox	Mark "D" Minicar
Mark 9E/4	4-speed gearbox	Mark "D" Minicar (1959 four-seater model)
Mark 9E/3S	3-speed gearbox Uni-directional Dynastart	Mark "D" Minicar De Luxe
Mark 9E/4S	4-speed gearbox Uni-directional Dynastart	Mark "E" Minicar
Mark 9E/3SR	3-speed gearbox Dynastart reverse	Mark "D" Minicar De Luxe (optional extra)
Mark 9E/4SR	4-speed gearbox Dynastart reverse	Mark "E" Minicar (optional extra)

Engine fitted to the Mark "F" is the Villiers Mark 31A/4 Siba or 31A/4 Siba Reversing

Comparison of the 9E/3 engine (Fig. 38) with the 9E/3S (Fig. 20) and the 9E/3SR (Fig. 15) indicates the main differences in external appearance of engines with SIBA electrical equipment. The ignition coil is mounted externally on top of the gearbox cover, with a single control box for the uni-directional self-starter model and two control boxes where reverse switching is incorporated (although a single box embracing all controls and the ignition coil is also specified). Externally both the three- and four-speed gearboxes are similar but the position of the gearbox oil plugs are slightly different. The main difference internally (apart from the extra gear ratio) is that the three-speed box change is by direct selection and that of the four-speed box is sequence-operated or "indirect" (*see* Chapter II).

The complete "tractor" unit embracing the 9E engine is shown in Fig. 14 (*upper*) and (*lower*). This is attached by steel shackle plates (from the trailing arm) fitted to the rear of the gearbox and the underside of the engine. The shackle plate carrier bolts are mounted in rubber bushes. The front stub axle is fitted to the trailing arm, which itself is pivoted in phosphor-bronze bushes in the bottom of the main tube. Movement of the trailing arm is controlled by a coil spring and hydraulic shock-absorber unit. The complete unit bolts to the engine bulkhead via the steering head. This would, of course, never normally be detached. If it is necessary to work on the complete engine independently, this can readily be

Fig. 38. Manual Start Villiers 9E Engine

Cable attached to pull lever inside car. Cover plate detached to expose contact-breaker assembly.

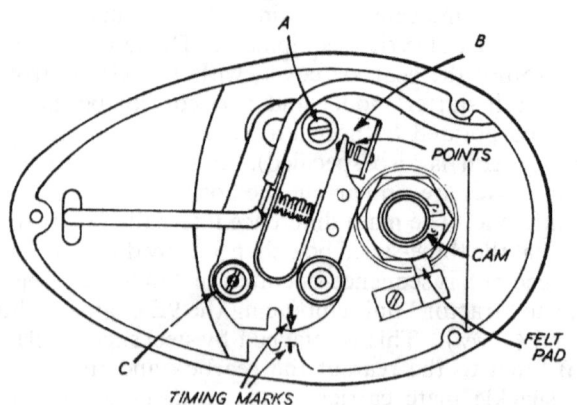

Fig. 39. Contact-Breaker on the Villiers 9E Engine

Adjustment is by slackening screw A and moving point bracket B to setting required. Slackening of screw C allows contact-breaker base plate to be moved for adjusting ignition timing (*see* text).

VILLIERS 9E AND 250 C.C. ENGINES

detached from the shackle plates and lifted out (after first detaching the silencer).

Access to the contact-breaker on the 9E/3 engine is by removing the small cover plate on the right-hand side of the engine. A drawing of the contact-breaker assembly is given in Fig. 39. The point bracket *B* is released by unscrewing screw *A*, when the point gap can be adjusted as

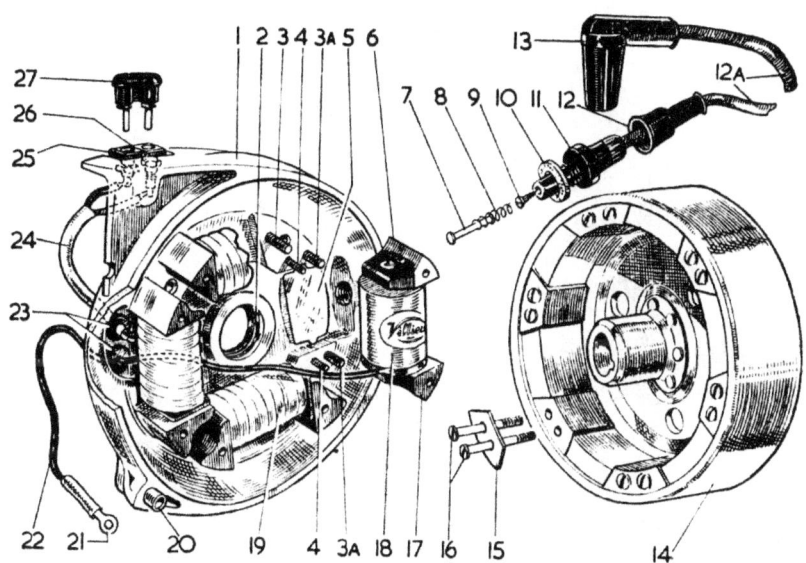

Fig. 40. Flywheel and Armature Plate

1. Armature plate
2. Oil seal
3. Screw, lighting coil poleshoe
3a. Screw, ignition coil poleshoe
4. Screw, ignition coil poleshoe
5. Insulating plate
6. Poleshoe, left-hand, H.T. coil
7. Pad, H.T. pick-up
11. H.T. terminal
12a. H.T. lead
14. Flywheel complete
15. Plate, poleshoe fixing
17. Poleshoe, right-hand, H.T. coil
18. Ignition coil
19. Lighting coil
22. L.T. lead, to contact breaker
23. Grommet
24. Lead, twin, lighting
25. Socket, small, lighting
26. Socket, large, lighting
27. Plug, twin, lighting

described in Chapter VI (with the engine turned so that the cam lifts the contact-breaker to its highest point). The recommended gap is 0·015 in.

To adjust the ignition timing only the contact-breaker unit is movable, the cam being keyed to the rotor, the rotor to the crankshaft. The procedure is to remove the cylinder head and set the contact-breaker points to the correct gap. Slacken off both the screws holding the contact-breaker base plate. Move the cylinder to a position exactly $\frac{7}{32}$ in. before top dead centre and then rotate the contact-breaker plate one way or the other until the points begin to open. Tighten up the contact-breaker base screws and re-check that the setting has not altered. The flywheel and armature plate are illustrated in detail in Fig. 40.

The contact-breaker unit on the 9E engine with SIBA electrics is

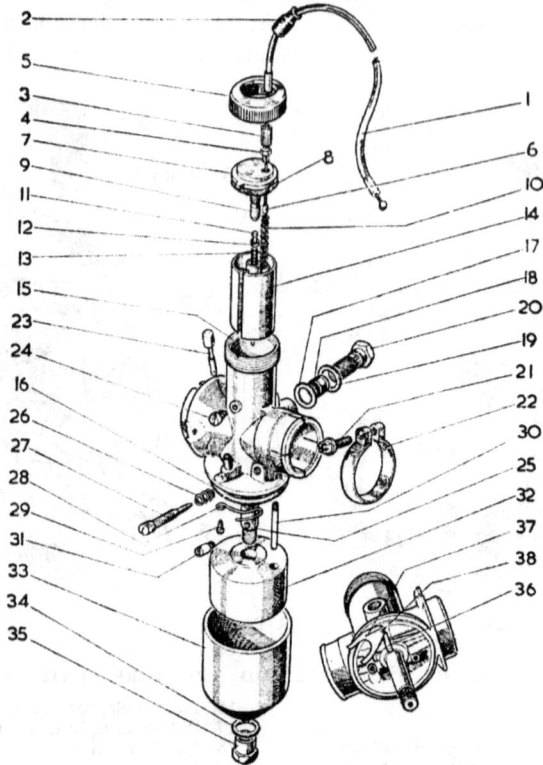

Fig. 41. Villiers S.25 Carburettor

1. Throttle cable
3. Cable adjuster
6. Cable nipple
9. Needle adjusting screw
11. Needle
14. Throttle
17. Banjo washer—small hole
18. Petrol filter
19. Banjo washer—large hole
22. Body clip
23. Tickler
24. Guide screw (throttle)
25. Centrepiece
27. Pilot jet needle
28. Tickler spring
29. Screw for tickler spring
30. Pilot jet
31. Main jet
32. Float
33. Float cup
36. Fuel needle
37. Fuel needle lever
38. Fuel needle lever pin

similarly reached by unscrewing the small cover plate on the right-hand side of the engine, *see* Figs. 15 and 67. These units are described in detail in Chapter XI, which should be referred to for data on gap setting and timing adjustment.

THE VILLIERS 9E AND 250 C.C. ENGINE

Both the 9E engine and the Mark 31A/4 engine are fitted with the Villiers S.25 carburettor (*see* Fig. 41). The top cable is connected to the carburettor slide, with an adjustment at either end of this cable. The second control is the choke cable, operating a butterfly shutter in the air intake. Again, adjustment is provided for at each end of this cable.

The taper needle fitted in the slide governs the fuel mixture, the recommended setting for this needle being 2·03 in. from the bottom of the slide to the end of the needle. This is the initial setting for the needle and no further adjustment should be required for a considerable period. Details of adjustment, etc., and dismantling the carburettor, are identical with the description already given in Chapter VI.

The clutch group is illustrated in Fig. 42. On later models the inner and outer clutch springs (*ref. Nos.* 5 *and* 6) are replaced by a set of nine

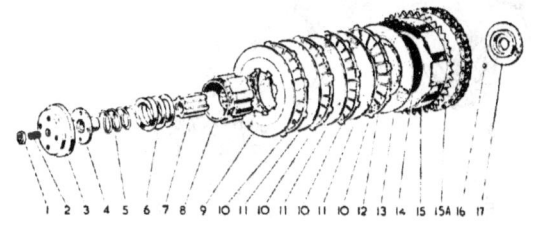

FIG. 42. CLUTCH GROUP

2. Clutch adjuster screw
3. Clutch cap nut
7. Clutch hub
8. Clutch sliding sleeve
9. Clutch pressure plate
10. Clutch driving plate

11. Clutch intermediate plate
13. Clutch back plate
15a. Primary drive chain
16. Rollers
17. Clutch chainwheel roller track

springs arranged radially and fitting in the sliding sleeve; otherwise this exploded drawing can be taken as typical of all models. Clutch adjustment is via a slotted screw under a hole in the gearbox cover plate (right-hand side of the engine), or alternatively at the push-rod end on the chain-case cover side (cover removed for access). Details of clutch adjustment are given in Chapter V, Section 1 (*also see* Figs. 15 *and* 16).

An exploded view of the three-speed gearbox as fitted to the Mark "D" is shown in Fig. 43. The four-speed gearbox as employed on the Mark "E" and Mark "D" four-seater (1959 version) is shown in Fig. 44. The complete engine is detailed in Fig. 45.

It is assumed that owners competent enough to tackle a complete stripping down of the engine for examination or overhaul, will be conversant with basic engineering requirements in this respect; therefore, description of the mechanical operations involved is unnecessary. The inexperienced owner would undoubtedly be better advised not to carry out any major overhauls himself but to have these undertaken by an authorized Dealer or Service Department.

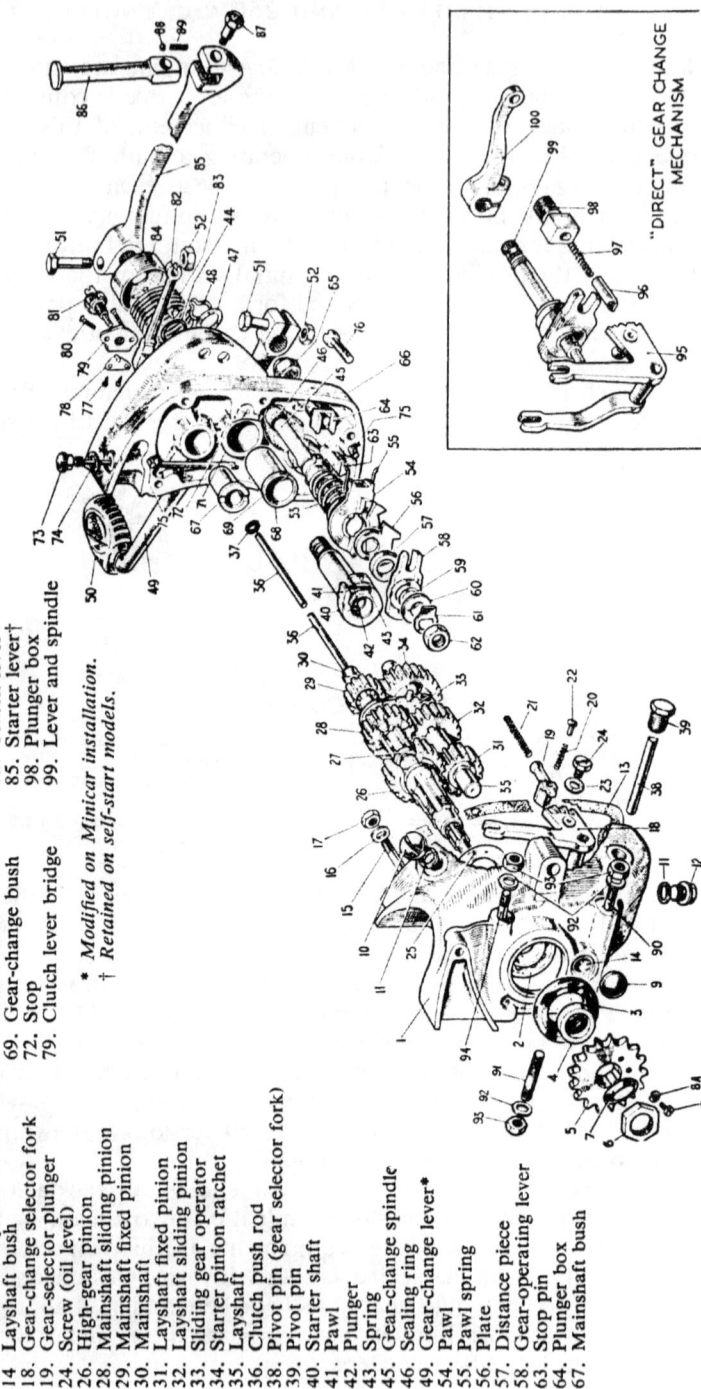

FIG. 43. THREE-SPEED GEARBOX

The "direct change" mechanism is employed on all three-speed boxes.

5. Final drive sprocket
14. Layshaft bush
18. Gear-change selector fork
19. Gear-selector plunger
24. Screw (oil level)
26. High-gear pinion
28. Mainshaft sliding pinion
29. Mainshaft fixed pinion
30. Mainshaft
31. Layshaft fixed pinion
32. Layshaft sliding pinion
33. Sliding gear operator
34. Starter pinion ratchet
35. Layshaft
36. Clutch push rod
38. Pivot pin (gear selector fork)
39. Pivot pin
40. Starter shaft
41. Pawl
42. Plunger
43. Spring
45. Gear-change spindle
46. Sealing ring
49. Gear-change lever*
54. Pawl
55. Pawl spring
56. Plate
57. Distance piece
58. Gear-operating lever
63. Stop pin
64. Plunger box
67. Mainshaft bush
68. Starter bush
69. Gear-change bush
72. Stop
79. Clutch lever bridge
82. Clutch lever
85. Starter lever†
98. Plunger box
99. Lever and spindle

* Modified on Minicar installation.
† Retained on self-start models.

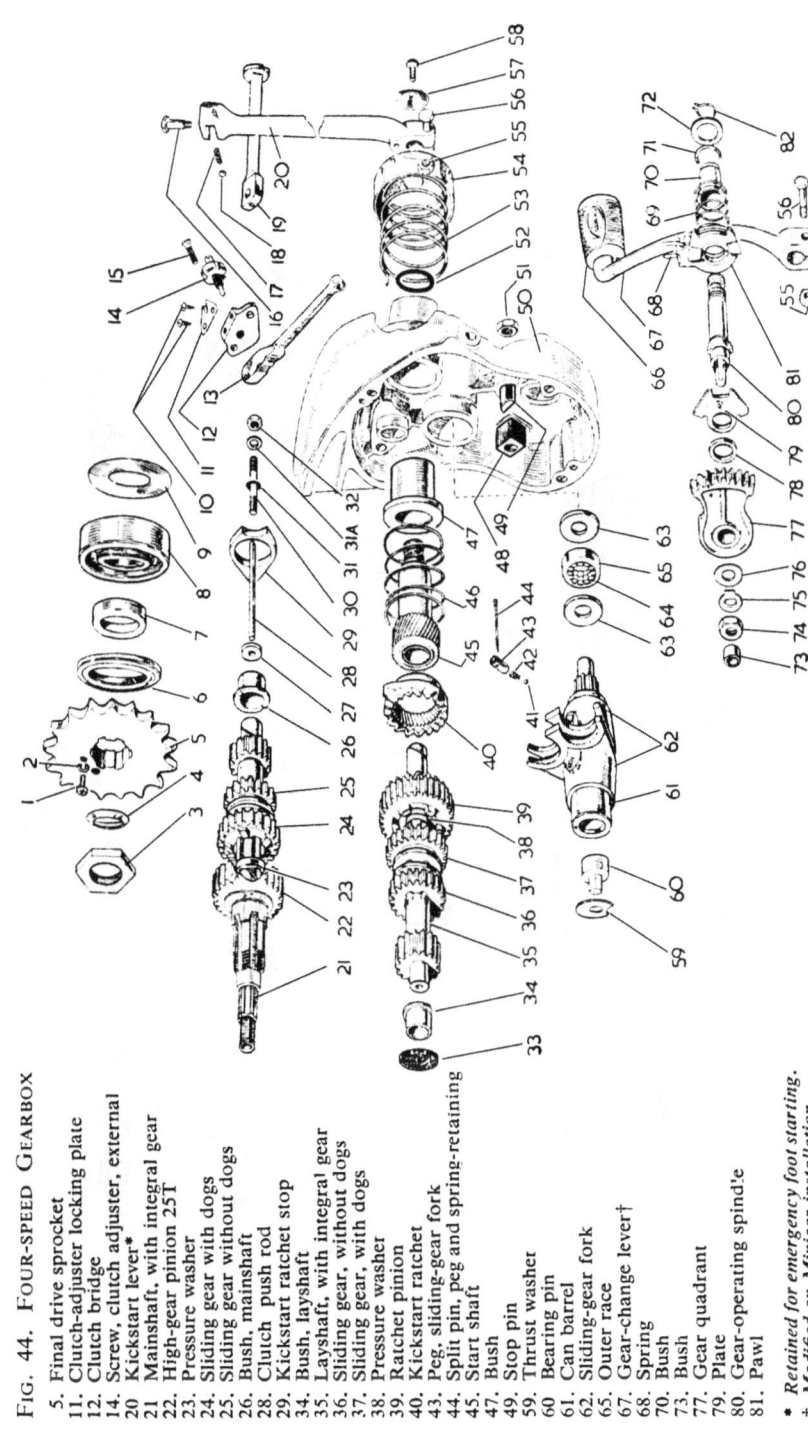

FIG. 44. FOUR-SPEED GEARBOX

5. Final drive sprocket
11. Clutch-adjuster locking plate
12. Clutch bridge
14. Screw, clutch adjuster, external
20. Kickstart lever*
21. Mainshaft, with integral gear
22. High-gear pinion 25T
23. Pressure washer
24. Sliding gear with dogs
25. Sliding gear without dogs
26. Bush, mainshaft
28. Clutch push rod
29. Kickstart ratchet stop
34. Bush, layshaft
35. Layshaft, with integral gear
36. Sliding gear, without dogs
37. Sliding gear, with dogs
38. Pressure washer
39. Ratchet pinion
40. Kickstart ratchet
43. Peg, sliding-gear fork
44. Split pin, peg and spring-retaining
45. Start shaft
47. Bush
49. Stop pin
59. Thrust washer
60. Bearing pin
61. Can barrel
62. Sliding-gear fork
65. Outer race
67. Gear-change lever†
68. Spring
70. Bush
73. Bush
77. Gear quadrant
79. Plate
80. Gear-operating spindle
81. Pawl

* Retained for emergency foot starting.
† Modified on Minicar installation.

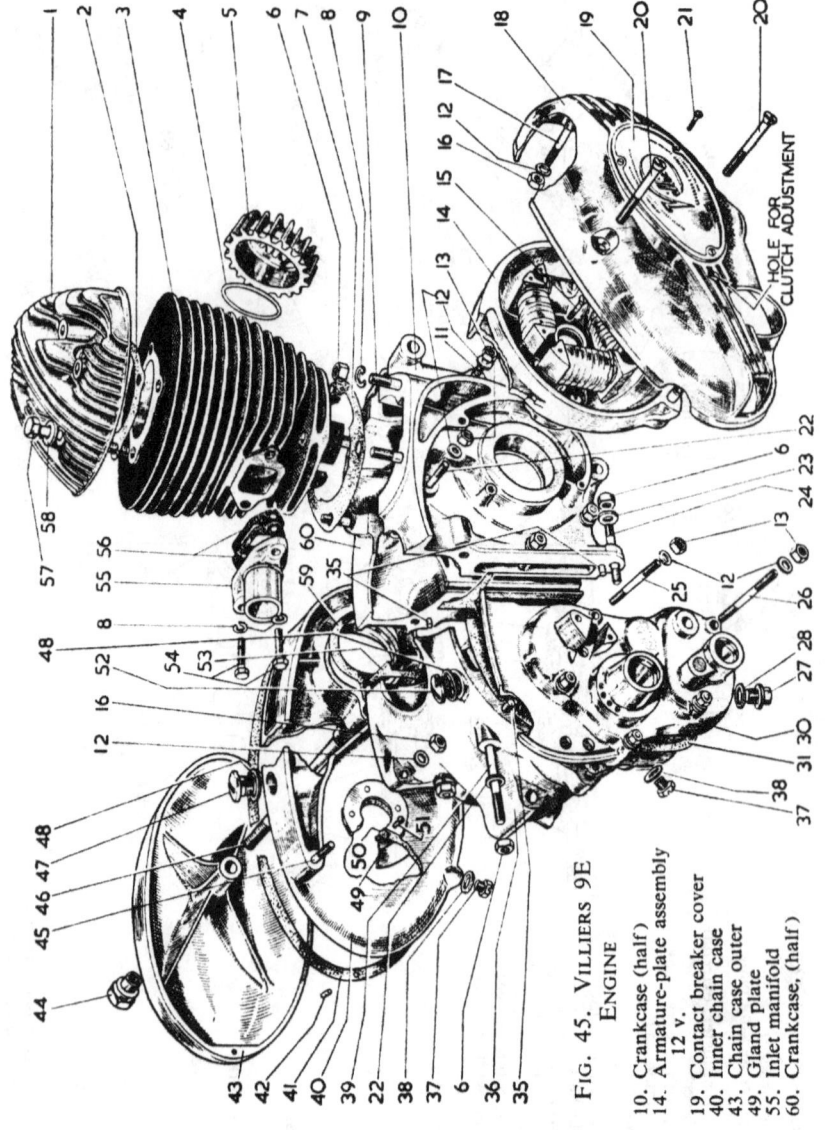

FIG. 45. VILLIERS 9E ENGINE

1. Crankcase (half)
14. Armature-plate assembly 12 v.
19. Contact breaker cover
40. Inner chain case
43. Chain case outer
49. Gland plate
55. Inlet manifold
60. Crankcase, (half)

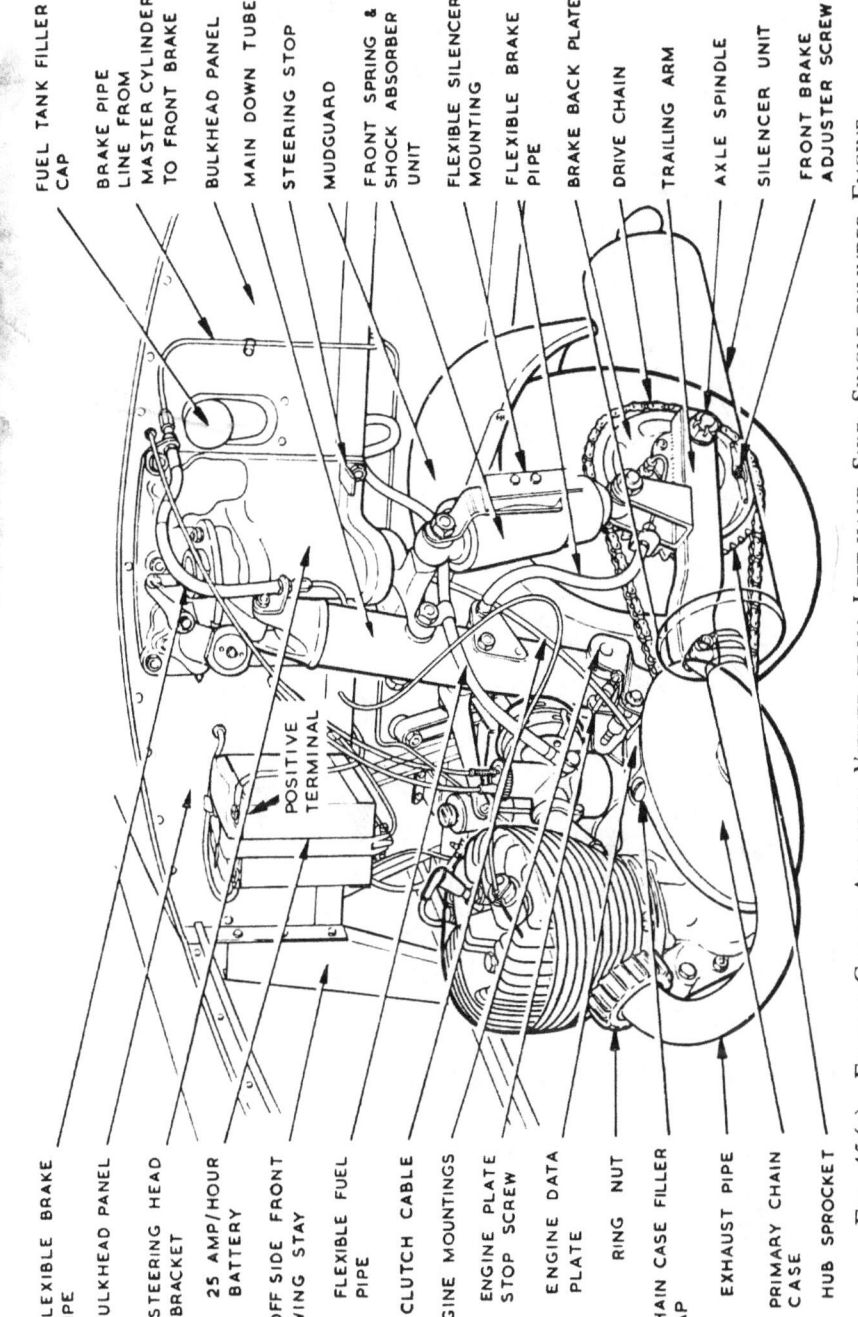

Fig. 45 (a). Engine Group Assembly Viewed from Left-hand Side, Single-cylinder Engine

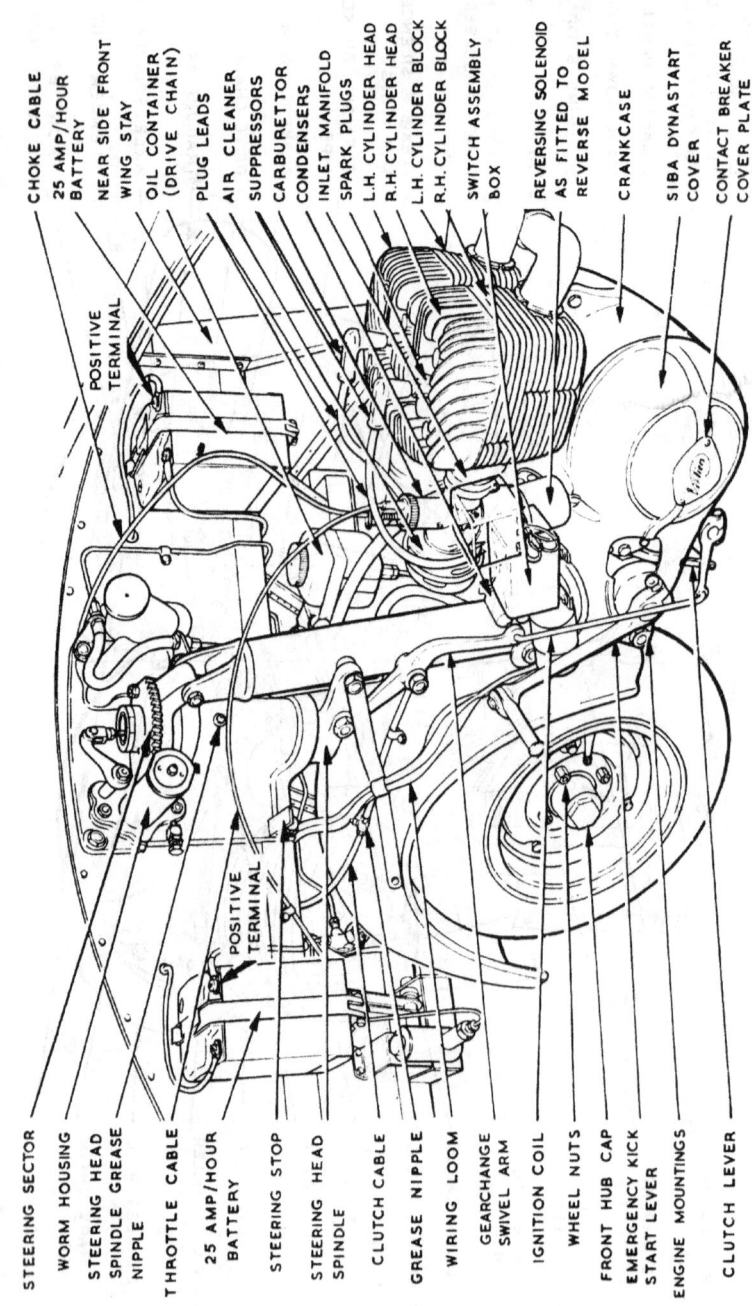

Fig. 45 (b). Engine Group Assembly Viewed from Right-hand Side, Twin-cylinder Engine

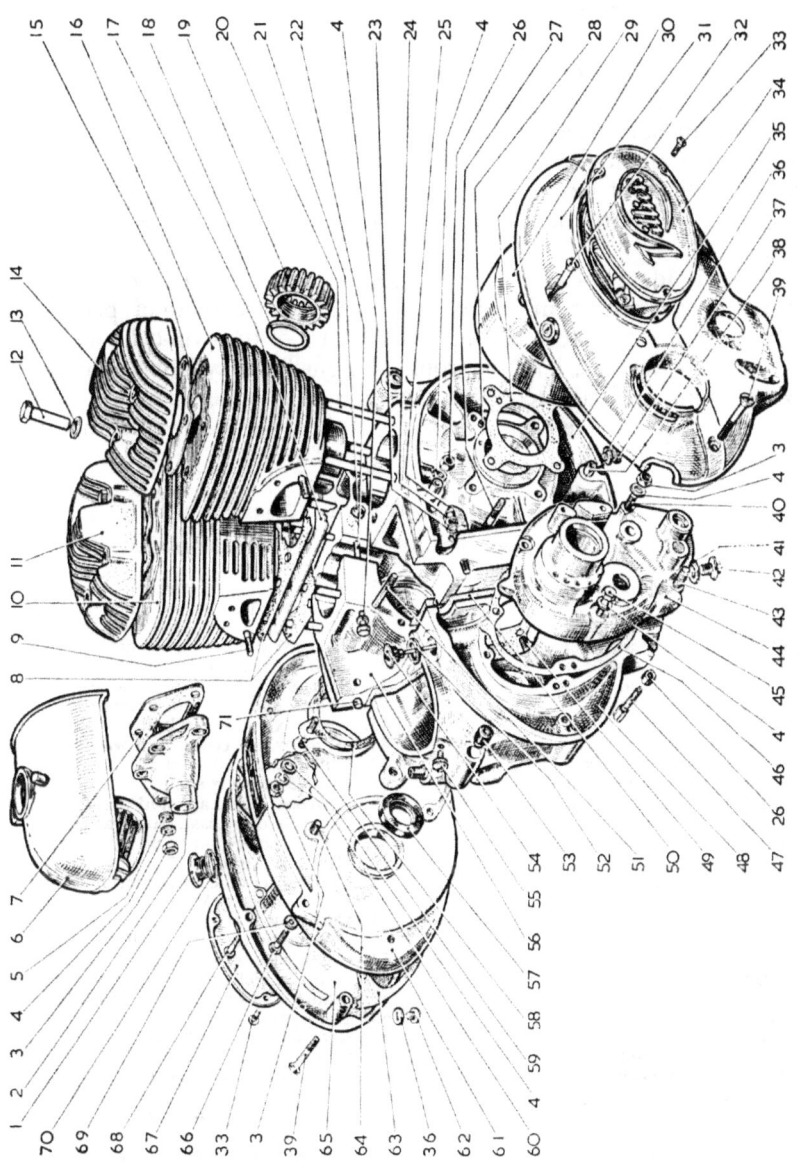

FIG. 45 (c). MARK 4T ENGINE GROUP   See Key page 74.

Installation details of the 250 c.c. Villiers single-cylinder engine and the 250 c.c. Villiers twin on Mark "G" models are shown in Figs. 45 (*a*) and 45 (*b*), respectively. General operating and maintenance instructions are essentially the same as for the 197 c.c. engine. The Mark 35A single-cylinder engine develops 11·5 B.H.P. at 4,500 r.p.m. The Mark 4T twin-cylinder engine, developed specially for the Bond Minicar is of identical displacement but faster revving, and develops 14·6 B.H.P. at 5,500 r.p.m. Both engines are fitted with a four-speed gearbox as standard, but the gear ratios are different (*see* Specifications). Both engines are available with either the standard Siba Dynastart or reversible Siba Dynastart (*see* Chapter XI).

Timing is identical on both engines, the contact-breaker points just beginning to open $\tfrac{5}{32}$ in. before top dead centre (with a permissible tolerance of 0·155 in. to 0·175 in.). In the case of the twin-cylinder engine it is usual to time the ignition from the right-hand cylinder. Since both sets of points are mounted on a common base plate this automatically sets the timing of the left-hand cylinder. It is possible however, that when

FIG. 45 (*c*) MARK 4T ENGINE GROUP

1. Chain case filler cap
2. Inlet pipe
3. Standard hexagon nut
4. Plain washer
5. Inlet pipe stud insulating washer
6. Carburettor and air filter group cover
7. Inlet pipe joint washer
8. Cylinder base joint washer
9. Inlet pipe fixing stud
10. Left-hand cylinder
11. Left-hand cylinder head
12. Nut for cylinder and head studs
13. Washer for cylinder and head studs
14. Right-hand cylinder head
15. Cylinder head joint washer
16. Right-hand cylinder
17. Cylinder plate joint
18. Exhaust pipe nut washer
19. Exhaust pipe nut
20. Cylinder and head fixing stud
21. Pinch bolt trunnion
22. Left-hand crankcase pinch bolt
23. Washer
24. Nut
25. Cable clip
26. Small hexagon nut
27. Crankcase fixing-stud
28. Armature plate dowel
29. Joint armature plate washer
30. Magneto assembly
31. Right-hand cover (less contact breaker cover and ignition switch)
32. Right-hand cover screw
33. Contact-breaker cover and left-hand nameplate screw
34. Contact-breaker cover
35. Right-hand crankcase (half)
36. Washer for drain and level screws
37. Drain screw
38. Right-hand crankcase cover dowel
39. Right-hand cover and chain case screw
40. Long stud for gearbox end cover
41. Gearbox drain plug washer
42. Gearbox drain plug
43. Short stud for gearbox end cover
44. Bushed end cover for gearbox
45. Gearbox end cover bolt
46. Gearbox end cover joint washer
47. Clutch cable adjuster
48. Bushed gearbox shell
49. Gearbox/crankcase stud
50. Gearbox/crankcase joint washer
51. Crankcase aligning stud
52. Dipstick washer
53. Gearbox/crankcase mounting lug bush
54. Gearbox dipstick
55. Carburettor cover screw
56. Left-hand crankcase (half)
57. Chain case oil seal
58. Crankcase/chain case joint washer
59. Fixing stud for rear half of chain case
60. ¼-in. spring washer
61. Rear half of chain case
62. Chaincase oil level screw
63. Chaincase joint washer
64. Fixing screw
65. Front half of chain case
66. Fixing screw for gearbox/chain case
67. Left-hand nameplate cover
68. Short screw for front half of chain case
69. Screw washer
70. Filler cap washer
71. Gearbox dowel

THE VILLIERS 9E AND 250 C.C. ENGINE

the timing is set by the right-hand cylinder the timing on the left-hand cylinder may not correspond when checked. If this is so the contact breaker base plate must be adjusted to bring the timing of both cylinders within the permitted tolerance.

The carburettor is a Villiers type S25, differing only in the size of main jet on the two engines. The single-cylinder engine or S25/8 carburettor is fitted with a 150 c.c. main jet. After 1,000 miles running it is recommended that this be replaced by a 130 c.c. jet. The S25/11 carburettor fitted to the Mark 4T engine is fitted with a 200 c.c. main jet.

Slow running adjustment is provided by the largest of the knurled screws in the body of the carburettor. The correct procedure for adjustment of slow running is to lift up the rubber sleeve and release the lock-nut on the throttle cable adjuster so that the adjuster can be screwed in to obtain slack on the cable. With the engine running and warm, the small spring-loaded knurled screw (which acts as a throttle stop adjuster) is screwed in until the engine will run at a speed just sufficient to prevent stalling. The slow running adjustment should then be screwed in or out until smooth running is obtained—readjusting the throttle stop, as necessary to adjust the actual idling speed achieved. Finally unscrew the throttle cable adjuster until there is approximately $\frac{1}{8}$ in. of free end movement on the outer cable and secure with the locknut.

If the mixture requires adjustment for normal running—e.g. the engine has a tendency to four-stroke when pulling, indicating too rich a mixture—this is done by altering the length of the needle in relation to the slide. Remove the air cleaner, followed by the annular ring from the top of the carburettor body and then withdraw the throttle slide and needle. The correct length of needle from the base of the slide to the end of the taper of the needle is 1·95 in. Adjustment of needle length is provided by a screw in the top of the slide. Screwing this screw into the body of the slide lengthens the needle and weakens the mixture; unscrewing the adjuster shortens the needle and richens the mixture. The effect is quite marked and any adjustments of this type should be made with only a quarter of a turn or less at a time.

CHAPTER IX

MODIFICATIONS

THE modifications listed and described in this chapter are based on the official modifications specified by Sharp's Commercials Ltd., the aim being to adapt early production models to later standards or to incorporate engineering improvements found by experience to offer certain advantages or overcome certain limitations. They apply particularly to the Mark "A" and Mark "B" models and the earlier Mark "C"s.

As to the extent by which an early model Minicar will benefit by modification to later standards, that is largely bound up with the actual condition of the vehicle at the time. In many cases—possibly most—extensive reworking of a Mark "A" or Mark "B" model will not justify the time or expense involved. Damage repair may also enter into the question, which, as far as bodywork is concerned, is covered briefly in Chapter V.

Conversion of Mark "A" Models to Rack-and-pinion Steering. This modification converts the early Mark "A" with cable-and-bobbin steering to the rack-and-pinion type of steering box, which subsequently became standard for the Mark "A" and Mark "B." Conversion parts were made available as a complete set, but some additional work was required to accommodate the steering bracket and to reposition the petrol tank.

The old unit is removed by taking off the steering wheel, uncoupling the steering-cable adjuster, releasing the adjusting collar on the steering shaft and dropping the steering shaft outwards, and then withdrawing from the underside of the bulkhead. The following must also be removed—

  (i) gear-change shaft (uncoupling cables and drop arm);
  (ii) steering idler pulleys;
  (iii) pulley brackets;
  (iv) steering and gear-change top bearing bracket;
  (v) petrol tank;
  (vi) battery.

A hole must be cut in the bulkhead to accommodate the steering-box mounting bracket, the size and position of this hole being detailed in Fig. 46. The bottom edge of this hole should come $\frac{1}{4}$ in. below the bend line of the bulkhead. The steering-box bracket can then be lifted into place and holes marked for drilling to take the mounting bolts.

The new petrol tank can be located in position relative to the filler cap and outlet, by marking the holes required for the tank brackets at each side and then drilling.

The new position for the steering and gear-change top bracket is marked out as in Fig. 47, 11¾ in. from the inside edge of the screen on a line at

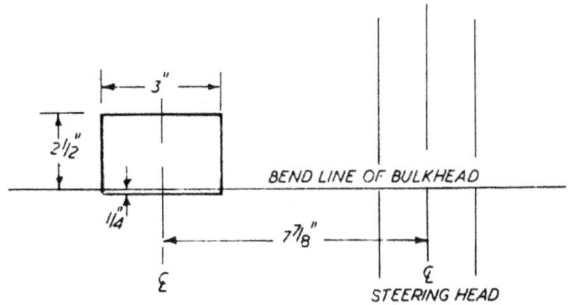

Fig. 46. Dimensions for Mounting New Steering-box Bracket
For rack-and-pinion conversion of early Mark "A."

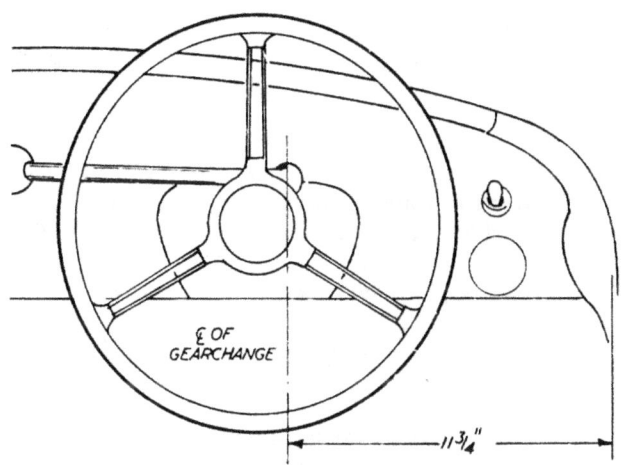

Fig. 47. New Position of Steering and Gear-change Top Bracket

right-angles to the bottom edge of the facia. A hole will have to be cut in the facia to accommodate the boss of the gear-change bush and the facia drilled for the necessary mounting bolts.

The new steering unit can then be assembled as follows. The steering-box mounting bracket is first fixed with ⅜-in. × ¼-in. B.S.F. bolts and the steering box mounted on the bracket with two 1½-in. × ¼-in. B.S.F. high-tensile steel bolts. The triangular-shaped steering plate is then secured to the bottom shackle bracket and locked with set screws. The rack and pinion steering ball joints are checked for alignment, finally tightening the ball-joint lock nuts.

The new petrol tank can now be fitted. Two of the new holes drilled will have passed through the battery carrier (which was why the battery had initially to be removed). Two countersunk bolts are used to hold the tank straps in these holes whilst the original fixing bolts can be used in the other holes. The battery can then be replaced.

The tapered end of the long shaft of the steering-shaft assembly is fixed in the steering box from the upper end and secured. Thoroughly grease the bushes in the top mounting bracket and place on the other end of the steering-shaft assembly. The top bracket can now be bolted in position on the facia. Finally fit the gear-change shaft, drop arm and cable, and the steering-wheel cap.

Modification to Front Stub Axle (Model B/10/1480 and subsequent models). The new stub axle adopted at this stage was strengthened by an increase in flange thickness to $\frac{5}{16}$ in. compared with $\frac{3}{16}$ in. on earlier models. From that date it was also issued as a standard spare and so, to fit it to vehicles earlier than Chassis Number B/10/1480, it is necessary to remove metal from the boss face of the fork adjacent to the stub axle flange, to a thickness of $\frac{1}{8}$ in. to compensate for the increased flange thickness.

Modification to Front and Rear Hubs (as from Chassis Number B/11/1545). As from the above model both front and rear hubs were machined to accommodate an additional ball bearing. The new-type hubs were also issued from that date as standard spares.

Modifications to earlier models, necessary to accommodate the additional bearing, required machining out the depth of the housing for the outer bearing to a further $\frac{5}{16}$ in. and the fitting of a new spacer tube ($\frac{5}{16}$ in. shorter).

Modification to Front Suspension Spring (as from Chassis Number C/2/1853). This change involved the replacement of the single front-suspension spring with a double-spring assembly consisting of two springs and two spring brackets. The new double-spring assembly could be fitted to earlier models, merely by elongating the $\frac{3}{8}$-in. diameter holes in the shock-absorber brackets to give clearance between the end of the bracket and the springs.

Introduction of Woodhead-Munroe Hydraulic Shock-absorber Spring Unit (as from Chassis Number C/4/1962). This was an entirely new unit introduced on production models in April, 1951, and also made available as a conversion set for earlier models. As a conversion set it was an

MODIFICATIONS

alternative to, not a replacement of, the double-spring unit described above. Basic details are given in Fig. 48.

Fitting of the Woodhead-Munroe unit entails removal of the complete engine assembly. With the engine unit free from the car, and the silencer unit detached, the suspension spring can be detached by removing its two

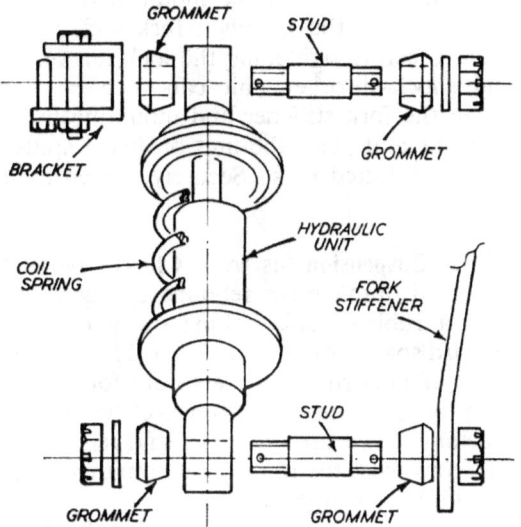

FIG. 48. WOODHEAD-MUNROE HYDRAULIC SHOCK-ABSORBER UNIT

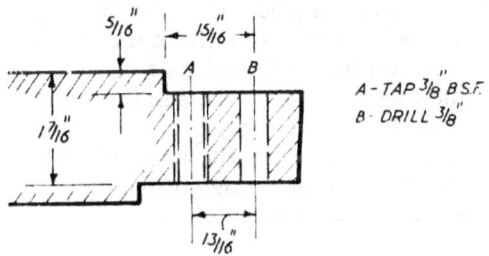

FIG. 49. MODIFICATIONS TO BOTTOM SHACKLE BRACKET

securing nuts. The fork stiffener is detached by unscrewing the large lock nut on the front hub spindle, the lock nut on the silencer support stud, and the nut at the top end of the stiffener. Next remove the nut from one end of the bottom shackle stud, and tap out and release the shackle bracket. Finally, remove the steering-head spindle and suspension-spring fixing stud from the bracket.

This bracket requires modification as shown in Fig. 49. Being of aluminium this can be worked readily with hand tools, if necessary. The original stud hole is then drilled out to ⅜-in. diameter. The suspension-spring stud on the fork is now redundant and this, too, should be reworked by filing down to the level of the casting.

The mounting bracket location is drilled and tapped ⅜-in. B.S.F. for the set screw, when the mounting bracket can be assembled. The steering-head spindle is then replaced and the modified bottom-shackle bracket fitted to the shackle. Fit the modified fork stiffener and re-set chain tension at this stage before tightening the lock nut on the front spindle. The spring and shock-absorber unit can then be tightened in their respective holes in the fork stiffener and mounting bracket. Finally, fit the rubber grommets and place the unit on fixing studs, and fit the flat washers and then the slotted nuts. Securely tighten these nuts and lock with split pins.

Independent Rear Suspension (as from Chassis No. C/12/2428). This modification rendered obsolete the rebound spring used on earlier rear-suspension units, a rubber buffer taking the place of this spring and becoming a standard spare from December, 1951. A complete conversion kit comprises a set of eight rubber buffers (four for each suspension unit).

Fitting is done by removing the rear wheel (with the vehicle suitably supported), detaching the metal dust cover and removing the suspension-spring adjusting screw from the top of the mounting bracket. The spring can then be prised off clear of the bracket.

The rebound spring is removed by unscrewing the fixing nut on top of the guide bar, and tapping the guide bar downwards, until there is sufficient clearance between it and the sliding block to withdraw the spring. One rubber buffer is then fitted in place of the rebound spring and the guide bar is repositioned and locked. Now check the hub for free upward and downward movement on the guide and slide bars.

To complete the assembly, load the inside of the suspension spring with three rubber buffers, fit the spring collar and remount the spring. Locate the spring and collar correctly, and tighten down the adjusting screw for the required degree of spring setting. This will normally correspond to a clearance of approximately ¼ in. between the collar and bracket.

Bonded-rubber Suspension. From the Mark "C" onwards the rear suspension is by bonded-rubber Flexitor units and a conversion set is produced for fitting to previous models without rear suspension (i.e. Mark "A" models).

In the case of models prior to A/11/254 the axle spindle will require modification by reducing the length of the 1-in. diameter spigot, until the end of the spigot is approximately $\frac{1}{16}$ in. below the face of the housing (when the spindle is fitted in the trailing arm, *see* Fig. 50.) In the case of models from Chassis No. A/11/254 to B/8/1279 inclusive, the original

MODIFICATIONS 81

hub-and-axle spindle is adaptable without modification. For all remaining Mark "A" models from B/8/1280 onwards the hub will require machining on the outer diameter to a flange of $5\frac{5}{8}$ in. diameter and $\frac{1}{4}$ in. depth to accommodate the new aluminium dust cover (*see* Fig. 51). Bolted rim-type wheels are fitted with the new suspension.

For fitting the Flexitor units the car should be raised to a convenient height above the ground in order to give access to the underside. The

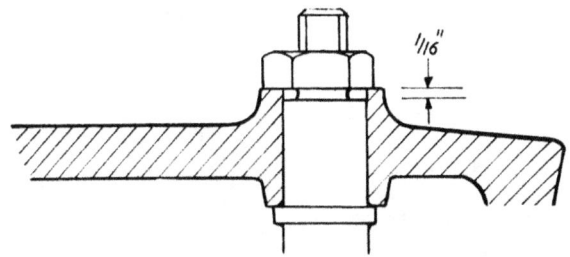

FIG. 50. REDUCTION OF AXLE SPINDLE TO TAKE BONDED-RUBBER REAR SUSPENSION UNIT

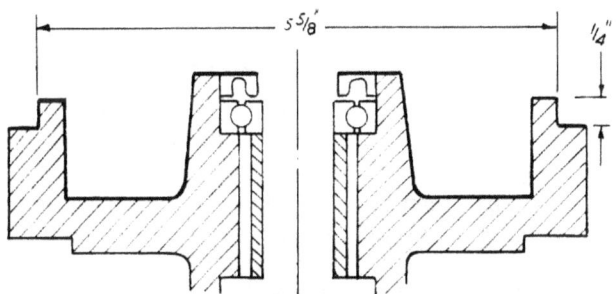

FIG. 51. MACHINING DIMENSIONS FOR HUB MODIFICATION TO TAKE NEW ALUMINIUM DUST COVER

brake rods are removed from the front linkage; the rods and guide brackets removed completely. The rear wheels and hub caps are also removed.

A stiffener plate has to be fitted across the floor. To position this plate correctly, drill a $\frac{3}{8}$-in. diameter hole $23\frac{1}{2}$ in. in from the offside edge of the floor panel and $1\frac{1}{4}$ in. back from the front line of rivets fixing the rear triangular bracing member (*see* Fig. 52). The floor stiffener plate can then be positioned squarely across the two rows of rivets with the hole in the plate aligned with the hole just drilled in the floor. Rivets covered by the plate should be removed; the plate can then be refitted by inserting the transfer lever pivot stud through the two holes with a ⅜-in. diameter flat washer over the short end, and securing the end protruding through the floor inside the axle channel with a nut. Using the holes from which rivets have been removed as a guide, drill $\tfrac{3}{16}$-in. diameter holes through the stiffener plate from the inside of the car and finish by securing the plate with 2 B.A. nuts and bolts, the nuts coming on the underside of the plate.

A section of the floor at each end of the axle channel must then be marked out as shown in Fig. 52 and cut away, e.g. with tinsnips. The

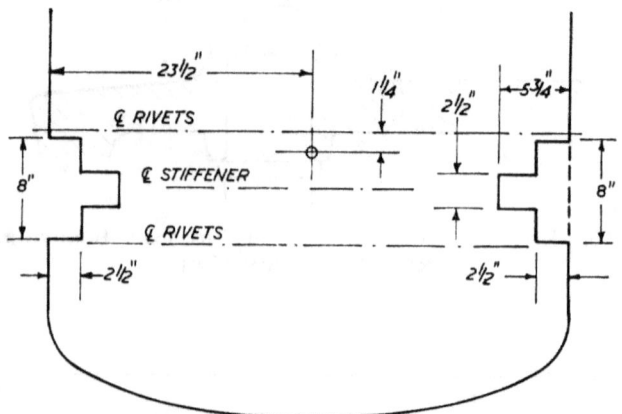

Fig. 52. Underside Plan showing location of Datum Hole for Stiffener Plate and Floor Cut-outs

Flexitor brackets can then be temporarily held in place and again rivets, covered by the base, marked and removed.

The carrier brackets can now be mounted firmly in each end of the axle channel, using 2 B.A. nuts and bolts (bolt heads to the outside). Each bracket must fit tightly against the top of the axle channel, preferably—to ensure this—being clamped in position whilst screwing up.

The base holes of the bracket can now be used as a guide for drilling $\tfrac{5}{16}$-in. diameter holes through the floor to accommodate the 1-in. × $\tfrac{5}{16}$-in. diameter fixing bolts, these being inserted, with a flat washer under the head, through the five rear holes and secured with a flat washer, spring washer and a nut.

Both axle spindles can then be fitted in their respective trailing arms, and brake shoes and hubs added. Both suspension assemblies are then fitted on to the base of their respective carrier brackets, and the units bolted in position, with a flat washer under the head of each bolt, and a flat washer, spring washer, and nut on the underside of the unit.

Finally, the brake linkage can be reconnected and adjusted, as necessary, to conform to Figs. 18 and 53. With the handbrake fully off, the transfer lever arm should lie at approximately 30 degrees to the transverse axis, as shown.

"Easistart" Decompressor. As from Chassis No. D/2/2703 the original cam-operated decompressor was replaced by a volumetric-type decompressor known as the "Easistart" unit on all manual-start models (up to and including the Mark "D"). The "Easistart" decompressor works on the principle of opening an additional head volume to the cylinder, thus decreasing the compression ratio and making the engine easier to turn over.

The "Easistart" decompressor can be fitted to all previous models without modification. The decompressor cable is detached from the

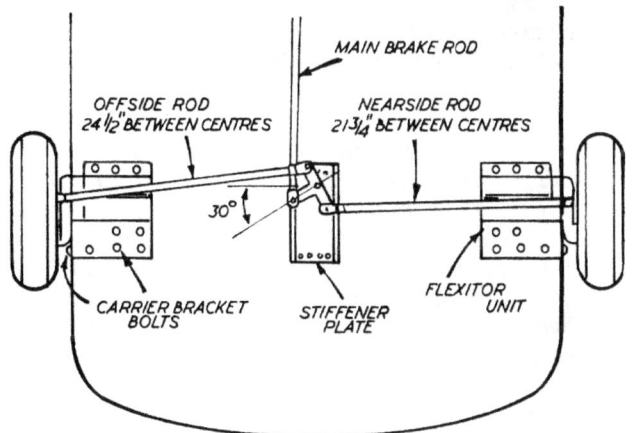

Fig. 53. Correct Assembly of Rear Brake Rods
See also Fig. 18 for useful data on brake system installation.

original unit and this unit unscrewed from the cylinder head. The "Easistart" decompressor then screws back in its place. The cable is reattached and adjusted to give approximately $\frac{1}{32}$ in. free end movement on the outer cable.

Top Engine-cradle Bolt (as from Chassis No. D/2/2703). The original modification to the top engine-cradle bolt was made at this stage, embracing a new bolt-and-shackle plate, the bolt now passing through the shackle plate and supporting the engine cradle on either side. It was subsequently supplied as a standard spare.

Models before Chassis No. C/2/1812 were originally fitted with the front fork, either drilled and tapped $\frac{3}{8}$-in. B.S.F. to take the top engine bolt (prior to Chassis No. B/5/850), or with the front fork merely drilled

(Chassis Nos. B/5/850 to C/2/1812 inclusive). Conversion sets differ in the bolt, cradle and bush.

In the case of the drilled and tapped fork, fitting of the conversion unit entails detaching the engine controls and removing the engine and cradle from the fork, with the bottom engine bolts still fixed in the rubber bushes. The top rubber bush in the cradle is replaced with the new bush. The $\frac{3}{8}$-in. diameter hole in the fork is drilled and tapped $\frac{7}{16}$-in. B.S.F. to a depth of $\frac{3}{4}$ in. and the engine bolt screwed into this full depth and locked with a $\frac{7}{16}$-in. lock nut. The engine unit is then fitted to the fork with a plain washer between the nut and a lock nut and washer fitted on the bolt, compressing the rubber bush. After fitting the shackle plate, release the lock nut to the face of the boss and finally tighten the top engine bolt.

Conversion of the drilled fork follows the same procedure except for drilling and tapping the $\frac{3}{8}$-in. hole oversize. Instead the $\frac{25}{64}$-in. hole in the fork is counter-bored $\frac{29}{64}$-in. to a depth of $\frac{9}{16}$ in., the $\frac{7}{16}$-in. lock nut run on $\frac{1}{2}$ in. from the start of the thread on the engine bolt, and the bolt fitted in the fork.

Engine Brace (all Mark "C" models after Chassis No. E/7/5799). All Mark "C" models from Chassis No. E/9/5800 to E/9/5966 were fitted with an additional engine brace to provide more even distribution of drive chain load. This fitting is readily mounted on earlier Mark "C" models. It is only necessary to remove the top left-hand nut from the side of the rear engine-mounting plate (viewed from the front) and the left-hand nut and washer from the rear of the cylinder block base, the brace being mounted between these two points and the nuts and washers replaced. Some slight readjustment of the carburettor position may be necessary to ensure that it clears the attachment.

Silencer Modification (as from Chassis No. E/4/5594). All Mark "C" Minicars subsequent to E/4/5593 were fitted with a straight-through type of silencer, this type also being supplied as a standard spare for Mark "A" and "B" models from April, 1953, onwards. Conversion sets are, however, necessary for fitting to Mark "A" and Mark "B" models, differing with each of these models.

Fitting simply requires inserting the reducing sleeve in the inlet end of the silencer and clamping tight with the bolt, fitting the mounting bracket loosely over the silencer body and attaching the silencer to the exhaust pipe. The silencer is then placed with the hole in the tailpipe pointing downwards, the exhaust pipe clamp bolt tightened up permanently and the supporting bracket fitted over the support stud with the fixing nut and silencer body clamp tightened.

Self-starter Set (Fig. 35). A self-starter set, suitable for fitting to existing standard models was introduced in 1952, utilizing a starter motor

MODIFICATIONS 85

mounted on the cylinder head and driving by means of a belt on to the engine flywheel (idling on a pulley when the engine is running). The fitting of a starter motor also entailed the use of a heavy-duty battery (6 volt, 57 ampere-hour). Complete details of this conversion are given in Chapter VII.

High-output Generator Set (Mark "C" Models after Chassis No. E/11/6111). The high output generator set which became standard on later Mark "C" models was made available in 1954 as a conversion set for fitting to Mark "A," Mark "B" and early Mark "C" models (up to Chassis No. E/11/6111). The conversion set comprises a new armature backplate complete with high output coils, high output flywheel, charge rate control switch and headlamp isolation switch. In addition standard 14/012 automobile cable is required for wiring the additional switches. Complete details of fitting the conversion set are given in Chapter X.

Braking System. The final braking system developed for the Mark "C" Minicar, for chassis numbers G-series onwards (from 1955 on), is produced as a conversion set for the adaptation of earlier Mark "C" models. Prior to Chassis No. F/5/6879, the handbrake was rod-operated and a handbrake cable is required in the conversion set. From Chassis No. F/5/6879 on, the handbrake is cable-operated and the existing cable can be adapted for the conversion merely by disconnecting the clevis end of the cable and repositioning the cable stop block to the new position required.

The basic arrangement of the late Mark "C" braking system is detailed in Fig. 18. Parts to be disconnected or dismantled on the original system are—

(i) The brake rod between the foot pedal and the cross shaft
(ii) The stop lamp switch clamp released from the rod
(iii) The handbrake unit (in the case of rod-operated handbrake only)
(iv) The intermediate lever and pivot stud are detached and the front brake cable-stop block released
(v) Detach the cross-rod shaft bearings and rods
(vi) Withdraw the split pin positioning the footbrake pedal on the common brake, clutch and accelerator pedal spindle
(vii) Withdraw the footbrake pedal from this spindle (necessitating removal of the nut on the spindle nearest the body panel and moving the spindle sideways).

To re-fit, the new torque rod (cross shaft) and its brackets are temporarily offered up in position, corresponding to the illustration, and fixing holes marked and drilled ($\frac{1}{4}$-in. diameter) in the floor. The brackets are then bolted in position (bolt heads on the inside of the floor). The new pivot stud is then fitted, bolting firmly to the floor. It will be necessary to enlarge the original $\frac{3}{8}$-in. hole to $\frac{7}{16}$-in. diameter and drill new holes for the fixing bolts.

The new push rod is then connected to the new intermediate lever, the threaded trunnion fitted in the short lever on the cross rod and the threaded end of the push rod tube screwed into the trunnion.

The intermediate lever can now be connected between the clevis end of the front brake cable; and the spacer, handbrake lever and intermediate lever mounted on the pivot stud, at the same time sliding the push rod into the push rod tube. The remainder of the assembly then follows in logical order. A $\frac{5}{8}$-in. diameter hole is required in the foot-well panel to clear the end of the footbrake and a $\frac{5}{16}$-in. diameter hole in the floor approximately $3\frac{1}{2}$ in. in and $\frac{1}{2}$ in. from the front edge of the floor to take the handbrake-stop block. Other leading dimensions conform to the drawing, the adjustment of the push-rod tube in the trunnion to give $6\frac{1}{2}$ in. between the centre of the trunnion and the centre of the clevis pin connecting the push rod to the intermediate lever, being important. This adjustment is locked by sliding a spacer tube over the end of the threaded portion protruding from the trunnion and tightening up the lock nut.

Details of brake adjustment, etc., will be found in Chapter V.

CHAPTER X

ELECTRICAL EQUIPMENT

Note: Colour coding of the wiring was adopted as standard for the Mark "C" circuit shown in Fig. 57 onwards. No standard code was used before this and coloured wires, where used, may be inconsistent. On Figs. 57–65(b), colours are indicated as follows—

    B: blue   *W:*   white
    LB: light blue   *GY:* grey
    BL: black   *G:*   green
    R: red   *P:*   purple
    Y: yellow   *BR:* brown

DETAILS of the magneto generator applicable to any particular model are covered in the chapter describing the Villiers engines. This chapter is concerned principally with the wiring systems used on the different models.

A wiring diagram appropriate to all Mark "A" models (and some early Mark "B" vehicles) is given in Fig. 54. The battery is a 6-volt Exide of 10 ampere-hour capacity mounted on the offside of the front bulkhead. The terminal block is fitted close to the battery, incorporating a fuse block mounting a 10-amp fuse. This fuse protects the lights, horn and windscreen-wiper circuits. The rectifier is mounted on the bulkhead beneath the petrol tank platform.

The block's end terminal on the battery side is connected to the battery. The centre terminal (immediately on the other side of the fuse) carries the lead from the magneto-dynamo and wires to the lighting switch and horn. The next terminal carries the earth lead of the ignition circuit and connects to the ignition switch. The remaining terminal carries the two rectifier leads and a lead from the generator-lighting coil.

An early change (1951) resulted in a modification of the lighting circuit. The design of the armature plate assembly on the Villiers engine was altered at this stage, both lighting coils being earthed internally and the two output leads connected internally, so that only one lead emerges from the armature plate (as opposed to three leads on the original version). The modified wiring diagram is shown in Fig. 55.

Differences are the connexion of the rectifier to the terminal block, with the single lighting coil output lead taken to the rectifier and not the terminal block. The rectifier case is also *insulated* instead of being earthed. The end terminal on the terminal block is not used.

This modification was incorporated on Chassis No. C/6/1974 and carried through to No. C/6/2138. The main service wiring and the ignition circuit is unaltered.

On Mark "B" models from Chassis No. C/6/2139 a further modified wiring diagram is used, Fig. 56. The battery and generator circuits remain the same but a new lighting switch, incorporating an ignition lock, is fitted. A dash light is also added to the circuit.

The wiring diagram for the early Mark "C" models remains substantially unaltered, the main difference being the addition of a tail stop-light controlled by a brake-operated switch. The tail light bulb in this case becomes a double-filament type with a different rating (*see* Fig. 57).

A limitation with these circuits is that, when the fitting of twin tail lights became obligatory, the demand when night driving was frequently in excess of the charging rate and so the battery gradually lost its charge, eventually needing an external recharge. Since the battery lighting side is divorced from the ignition circuit the engine can still be run with the battery removed. However, under such circumstances the rectifier should be disconnected entirely from the terminal blocks, removing the two appropriate leads (on the same terminal).

For emergency operation it is also possible to operate the lights direct from the magneto-generator on these circuits with the battery removed, although, of course, current will only be produced for the lights when the engine is running and the intensity of the lights will vary with the speed of the engine.

In the case of the original circuit (Fig. 54), the two rectifier leads are removed from the end terminal on the terminal block and left free. The generator lead, which goes to the *same terminal* as that from which the rectifier leads were removed, is also taken off the terminal and earthed, e.g. made off round the nut, on the screw holding the terminal block to the front bulkhead.

In the other three circuits described (Figs. 55–57), it is only necessary to remove the single generator lead attached to the rectifier case and connect to the *centre* or supply terminal on the terminal block.

A point which should be emphasized with all these emergency lighting circuits is that it may be possible to generate too much current by over-revving the engine and thus blow one or more of the light bulbs in the circuit. The limit to engine speed above which bulbs may be blown is the speed which gives an illumination from the lights equivalent to that obtained normally when the battery is in circuit.

The battery on the Mark "C" is mounted on a platform bolted to the nearside front wing and to the underside of the floor. The rectifier is mounted beneath the bulkhead, insulated from it by rubber grommets. The terminal and fuse block *are* mounted on the bulkhead near the rectifier. A 15-amp fuse is standard.

As from Chassis No. E/11/6151 a higher output generator is fitted and the wiring diagram for later Mark "C"s is modified as in Fig. 58. The

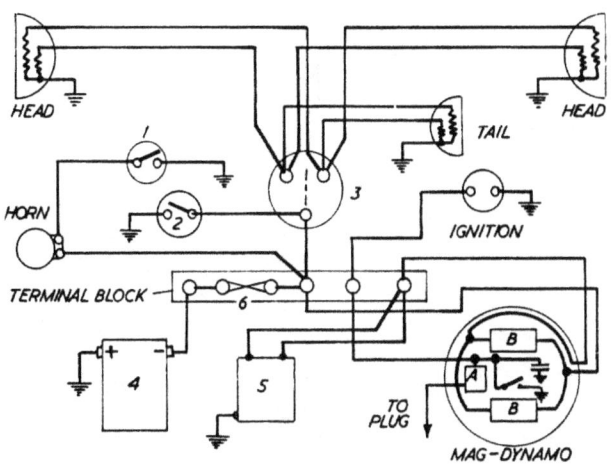

Fig. 54. Wiring Diagram Mark "A" Models and Early "B"

1. Horn button
2. Wiper motor (where fitted)
3. Lighting switch
4. 6-volt battery
5. Rectifier
6. 10-amp fuse
A. High-tension coil
B. Lighting coils

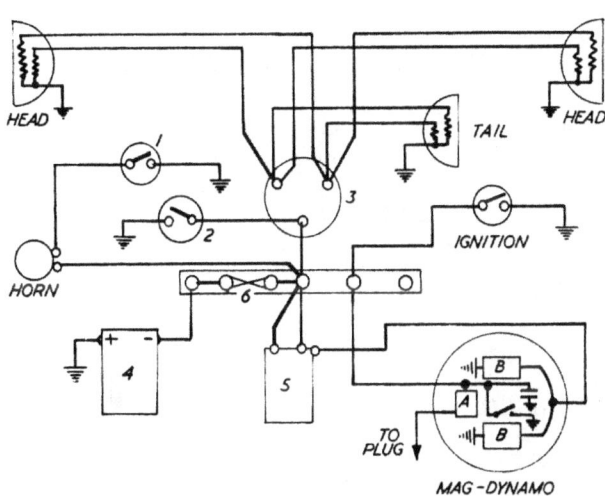

Fig. 55. Wiring Diagram Mark "B" 1951 Model

1. Horn button
2. Wiper motor (where fitted)
3. Lighting switch
4. 6-volt battery
5. Rectifier
6. 10-amp fuse
A. High-tension coil
B. Lighting coils

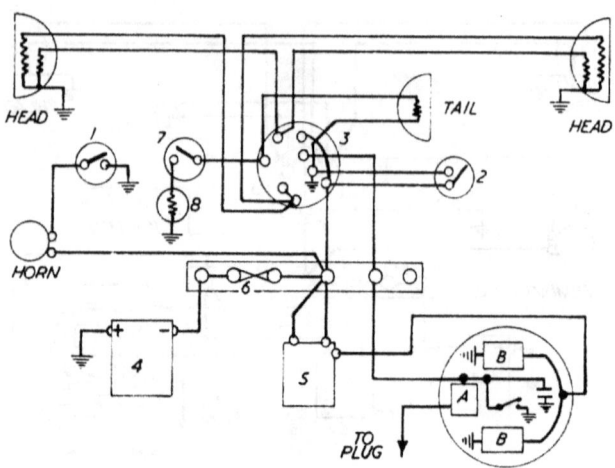

Fig. 56. Wiring Diagram Mark "B" (from Chassis No. C/6/2139)

1. Horn button
2. Wiper motor
3. Combined lighting and ignition switch
4. 6-volt battery
5. Rectifier
6. 10-amp fuse
7. Dash light switch
8. Dash light
A. High-tension coil
B. Lighting coils

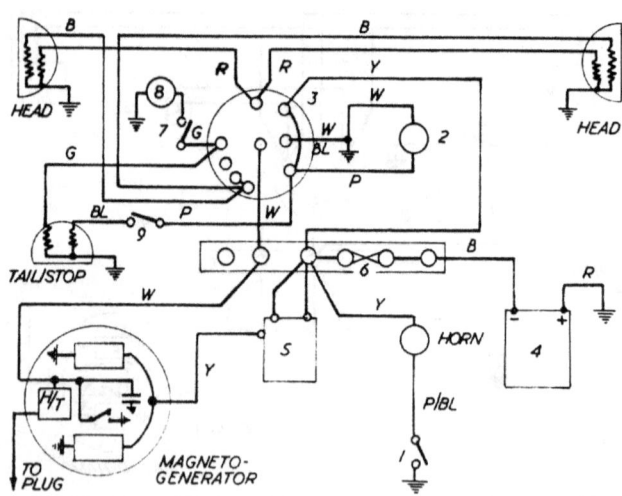

Fig. 57. Wiring Diagram Early Mark "C" Models

1. Horn button
2. Wiper motor
3. Combined ignition and light switch
4. 6-volt battery
5. Rectifier
6. 10-amp fuse
7. Panel light switch
8. Panel light
9. Stop light switch

rectifier case is now earthed and the circuit incorporates a push-pull switch for controlling the rate of charge. This switch is mounted directly above the speedometer head. With this switch pushed *in* the battery is receiving charge at a low rate; with the switch pulled *out* the battery is being charged at maximum rate.

Normally the high charge rate should be required only when running with lights, or when the battery has been allowed to get into a partially discharged position through excessive use. The makers specifically recommend running with the charge control switch *in* for normal daytime operation (when lights are not required), and with the switch *out* only when running at night with lights. There is a danger of the battery being overcharged and consequently damaged by running continuously with the control switch *out* (i.e. maximum charge rate).

If in doubt as to the condition of the battery it should be possible to judge the state of charge by switching on the lights with the engine stopped and then examining the brightness of the lights. A more positive check is to measure the specific gravity of the battery acid with a hydrometer (which is a relatively cheap instrument obtainable from most local garages).

A conversion set is put out for the fitting of the high output generator and magneto unit to early models (Mark "A," Mark "B" and early Mark "C") with either the Villiers 6E or 8E engine. This comprises a new armature back plate with high output coils, new flywheel, charge-rate control switch and a headlamp-isolation switch.

There are slight variations in this set according to the model to be converted. In the case of Mark "A" and "B" cars a shorter lead length is required than for a Mark "C" conversion. Also, if either set is to be fitted to a model already fitted with a self-starter (which may have been added as extra equipment), a different-type terminal is fitted to one of the leads; and the charge control switch is not used, since the heavy-duty battery associated with starter-motor equipment has sufficient capacity to accommodate a normal maximum charge rate. The standard Mark "C" conversion set can, however, be adapted to any model by cutting the leads to length, if necessary (e.g. for a Mark "A" or Mark "B" car) and/or fitting the different type of terminal if a car with a starter motor is involved.

The wiring diagram as given in Fig. 58 applies for the conversion of standard models. For the conversion of any model already fitted with a self-starter the wiring diagram is shown in Fig. 59; this is identical but for the addition of the starter-motor circuit and the elimination of the charge-rate control switch, on the basis that the starter-motor demand will ensure that the battery is never likely to become overcharged operating continuously at the maximum charge rate.

Fitting the conversion set is relatively straightforward. If a self-starter is already fitted, the starter drive belt and also the loose pulley must be

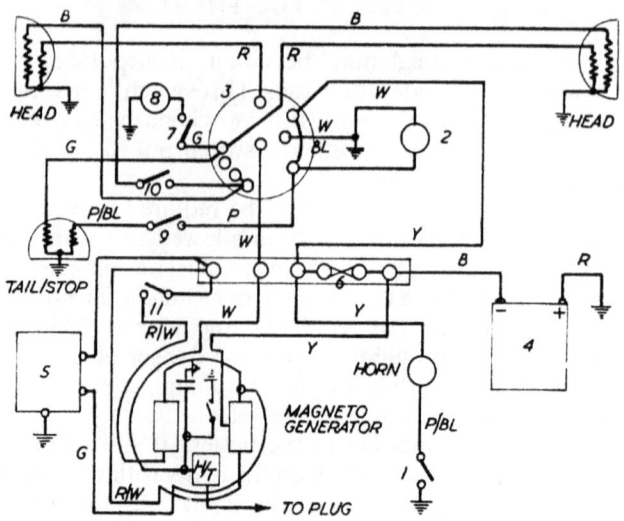

Fig. 58. Wiring Diagram Mark "C" with Higher Output Generator (from Chassis No. E/11/6151)

1. Horn button
2. Wiper motor
3. Combined ignition and light switch
4. 6-volt battery
5. Rectifier
6. 15-amp fuse
7. Panel light switch
8. Panel light
9. Stop light switch
10. Headlamp isolator switch
11. Charge rate control switch

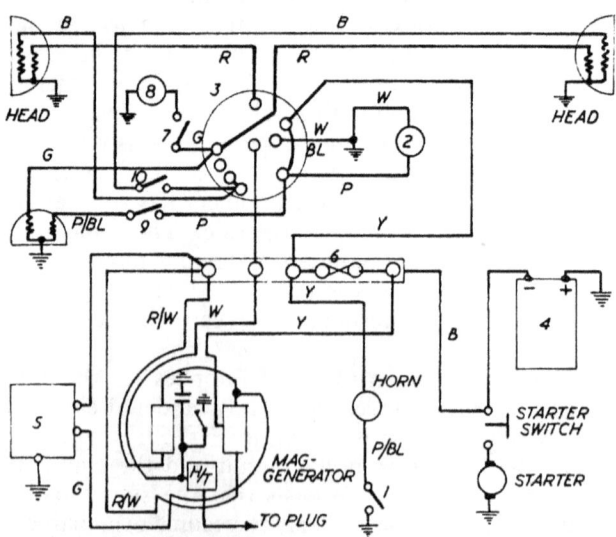

Fig. 59. Wiring Diagram Mark "C" with Self-starter
Note the charge rate control switch is eliminated and battery capacity increased.

removed and the stud unscrewed from the flywheel nut. On all models the original flywheel can then be removed.

The leads from the armature back plate are disconnected from the terminal block and the wiring clips loosened. The four screws holding the armature back plate are then removed and the back plate is withdrawn, tapping, if necessary, with a block of wood to release it. The new backplate is fitted and tapped into place and held with the four screws. The new flywheel is then fitted and the timing and contact breaker adjusted as necessary (*see section on ignition adjustment*, Chapters VI and VIII).

To prepare for the new fittings a ½-in. diameter hole must be drilled in the facia panel (directly above the speedometer head for standard position) to take the charge-rate control switch (omit this on cars fitted with a starter motor where this switch is not used). Another ½-in. diameter hole must also be drilled on the facia to take the headlamp-isolation switch, a convenient position being slightly to the left of the steering wheel.

The rectifier, if insulated, must be unbolted, the rubber grommets removed and the unit remounted without the grommets so that it is effectively earthed. The wiring is then completed by connecting the armature back-plate leads to the terminal block in accordance with the wiring diagram, and completing the wiring to the switches with standard 14/012 automobile cable. The lead from the offside side-lamp filament is detached from the common side-lamp terminal on the lighting switch and attached to the tail-lamp terminal, so that the headlamp isolation switch now provides a separate control to the offside headlamp.

It is possible to take advantage of the higher output generator by increasing the power of the headlamp bulbs which can be of 18/3-watt size, as standard on the later Mark "C" models. In this case the rating of the fuse should be increased, replacing the original 10-amp fuse with one of 15-amp capacity.

A standard wiring diagram for Mark "C" De Luxe models fitted with self-starter is shown in Fig. 60. This applies to models from Chassis No. F/9/7414. On all Mark "C" models with electric starter the motor is mounted on a bracket fitted on the cylinder-head studs and operated by a "pull" control switch, connected by cable to the starter switch located on the underside of the bulkhead panel. The drive from the starter motor to the engine is by a Vee-belt. When the starter is operated, the belt runs off the loose pulley on which it is mounted on to the flywheel rim and thus drives the engine. This loose pulley has to be removed (after first transferring the belt to the flywheel rim) to gain access to the contact-breaker assembly for adjustment, etc.

All subsequent models (i.e. Marks "D," "E," "F," "G") employ a 12-volt electrical system. A wiring diagram for the standard Mark "D" is shown in Fig. 61. The two batteries, each of 6 volts 12 ampere-hour capacity, are connected in series and mounted on a carrier bolted to a platform beneath the rear of the nearside front wing on the Mark "D,"

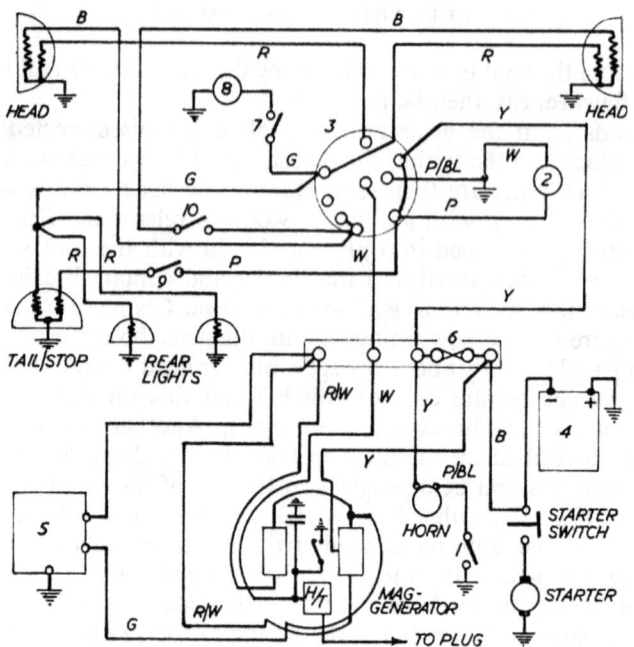

FIG. 60. WIRING DIAGRAM LATER MARK "C" DE LUXE

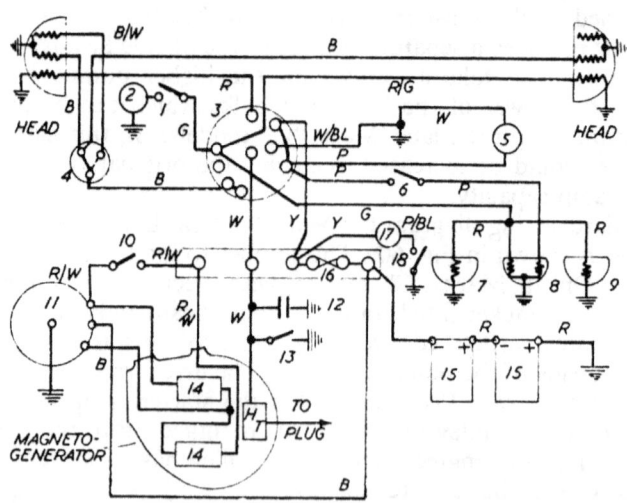

FIG. 61. WIRING DIAGRAM FOR MARK "D" STANDARD

1. Panel light switch
2. Panel light
4. Dip switch
5. Wiper motor
6. Stop light switch
7, 9. Tail lights
8. Stop and number plate light
10. Charge rate control switch
11. Rectifier
12. Condenser
13. Contact breaker
14. Lighting coils
15. 6-volt battery (two in series)
16. 15-amp fuse

or on the bulkhead on the Mark "E." Again the positive side of the series connexion is earthed. A charge rate control switch is retained on the facia immediately above the speedometer. The rectifier is mounted on the bulkhead underneath the petrol tank platform on the offside,

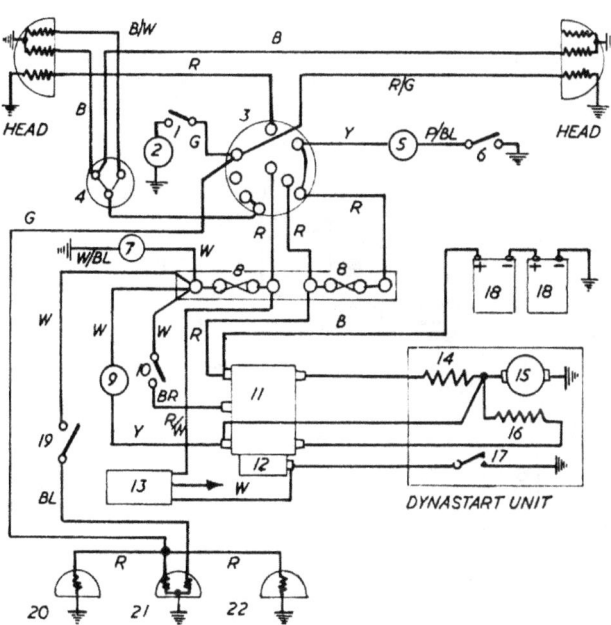

FIG. 62. WIRING DIAGRAM MARK "D" WITH UNI-DIRECTIONAL DYNASTART UNIT

1. Panel light switch
2. Panel light
3. Main switch
4. Dip switch
5. Horn
6. Horn button
7. Wiper motor
8. 15-amp fuses
9. Ignition warning lamp
10. Starter switch (button)
11. Switch assembly box
12. Condenser
13. Coil
14. Series winding
15. Armature
16. Shunt winding
17. Contact breaker
18. 6-volt batteries (connected in series)
19. Stop light switch
20, 22. Rear lights
21. Stop and number plate light

adjacent to the terminal block. The centre bolt of the rectifier is earthed to the bulkhead.

The De Luxe Mark "D" with self-starter incorporates a SIBA Dynastart unit, embracing generator and starter. Charge rate is automatically controlled by the regulator on a constant-voltage basis, the system in this case being essentially the same as in normal car practice. An ignition coil is mounted separately from the unit and also a switch box (on the Dynastart unit). The appropriate wiring diagram is shown in Fig. 62.

It will be noted that all the Dynastart units employ a negative earth.

Where a reverse gear is fitted a Dynastart Reversible unit is fitted, the wiring being as in Fig. 63. The reverse unit incorporates two contact breakers, one for forward running and the other for reverse (reversing the direction of rotation of the engine), also an additional switch box

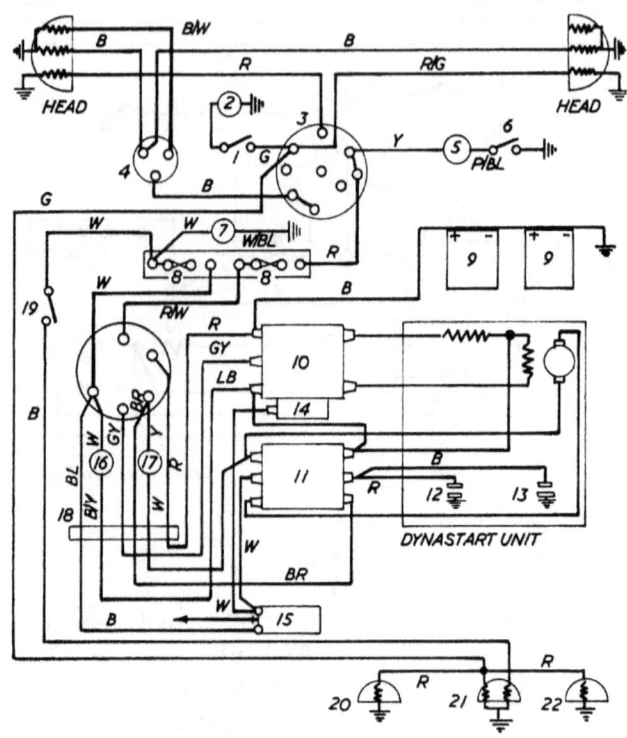

FIG. 63. WIRING DIAGRAM MARK "D" WITH DYNASTART REVERSE

9. 6-volt batteries (connected in series)
10, 11. Control switch boxes
12. Reverse contact breaker
13. Forward contact breaker
14. Condenser
15. Coil
16. Forward indicator lamp
17. Reverse indicator lamp
18. Six-pin plug and socket

(*See* Fig. 62 for key to other numbers.)

mounted externally. The circuit is further elaborated by the fact that warning lamps are introduced to provide a visual indication of whether "forward" or "reverse" drive is selected. Operating technique is fully described in Chapter II, whilst Chapter XI follows the details of both the Dynastart uni-directional and Dynastart reversible units.

Wiring diagrams appropriate to Marks "E" and "F" with uni-directional Dynastart are shown in Fig. 64, and with Dynastart reverse in

ELECTRICAL EQUIPMENT 97

Fig. 65. The control box in the case of the latter comprises combined voltage regulator, cut-out, starter contactor, reversing contactor and ignition coil. An additional circuit not found on earlier models is the

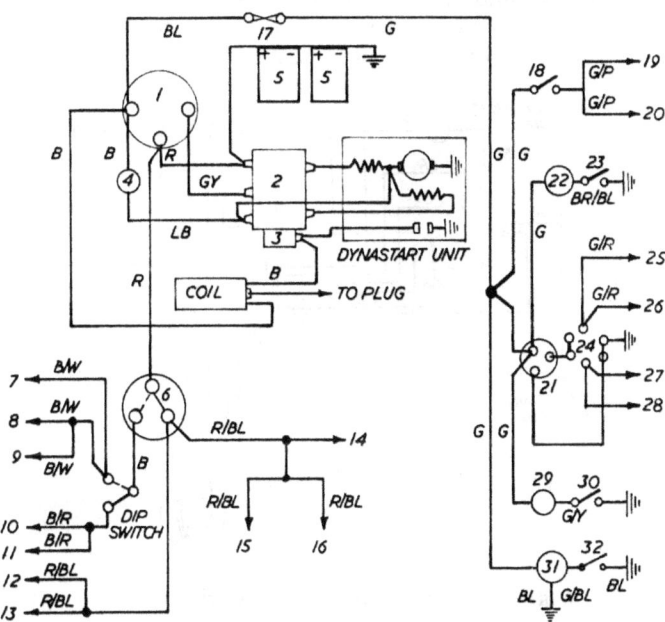

Fig. 64. Wiring Diagram Marks "E," "F" and "G" with Uni-directional Dynastart

1. Starter and ignition switch
2. Control box
3. Condenser
4. Ignition warning light
5. 6-volt batteries (connected in series)
6. Light switch
7. Main beam warning light
8. R.-h. head main beam
9. L.-h. head main beam
10. R.-h. head dip beam
11. L.-h. head dip beam
12. L.-h. sidelight
13. R.-h. sidelight
14. Number plate lamp
15, 16. Tail lights
17. Fuse
18. Stop lamp switch
19. 20. Stop lamps
21. Flasher unit
22. Horn
23. Horn button
24. Flasher switch and warning light
25. L.-h. rear flasher
26. L.-h. front flasher
27. R.-h. front flasher
28. R.-h. rear flasher
29. Neutral indicator lamp
30. Neutral indicator lamp switch
31. Wiper motor
32. Wiper motor switch

flashing light indicators for front and rear, operated by a dash-mounted switch.

Little attention should be required by the electrical equipment, other than items covered in the chapter on regular maintenance. The battery acid level should normally be inspected weekly and topped-up with distilled water, if necessary. Vent plugs should be screwed up tight and the exterior of the battery kept clean and the terminals coated with petroleum jelly to prevent corrosion.

The starter motor is lubricated by a grease nipple fitted in the bearing cover plate and should receive attention with a grease gun about every 500 miles. The windscreen-wiper motor is packed with grease and should require no further lubrication or adjustment throughout its life. The

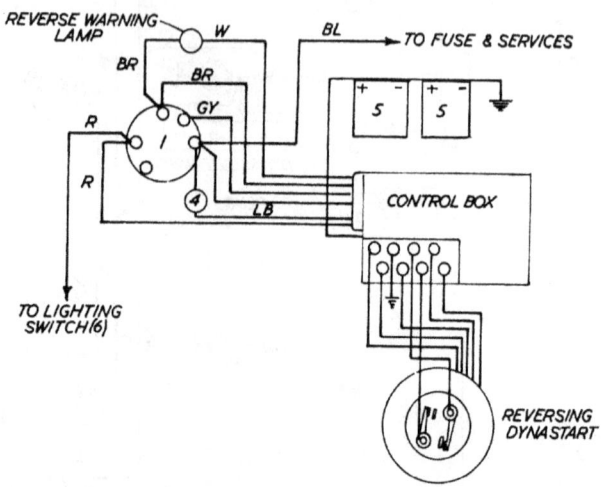

FIG. 65. WIRING DIAGRAM MARK "E" WITH DYNASTART REVERSE
Only the wiring to the starter and ignition switch differs. The circuits are identical with Fig. 64 as regards the service circuits.

wiper spindle can be lubricated occasionally, with a drop or two of oil, where it emerges from the windscreen.

Adjustment and/or replacement of light bulbs is as follows—

Models Mark "A" and "B." Head and sidelights are combined in a double-filament bulb. To reach the bulb, unscrew the cheesehead set screw on the lamp rim, when the glass and reflector can be removed from the lamp body. The tail-light bulb is removed by unscrewing the cover.

Adjustment of the headlamps is made by slackening the holding nut inside the body, when the lamp may be swivelled to any position.

Mark "C." Head and sidelights are combined in a double-filament bulb. Two adjustable set screws on the lamp rim hold the reflector and glass, allowing the latter to be removed from the lamp body when unscrewed.

These set screws also provide the beam adjustment. Unscrewing the

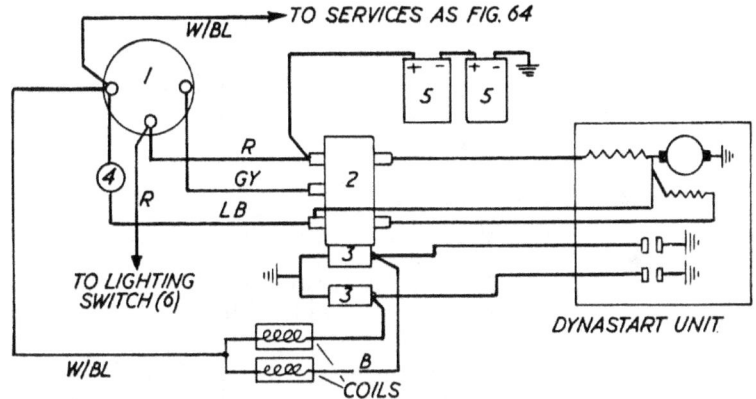

Fig. 65 (a). Wiring Diagram Mark "G" Twin with Undirectional Dynastart

Wiring to the services is the same as that of Fig. 64.

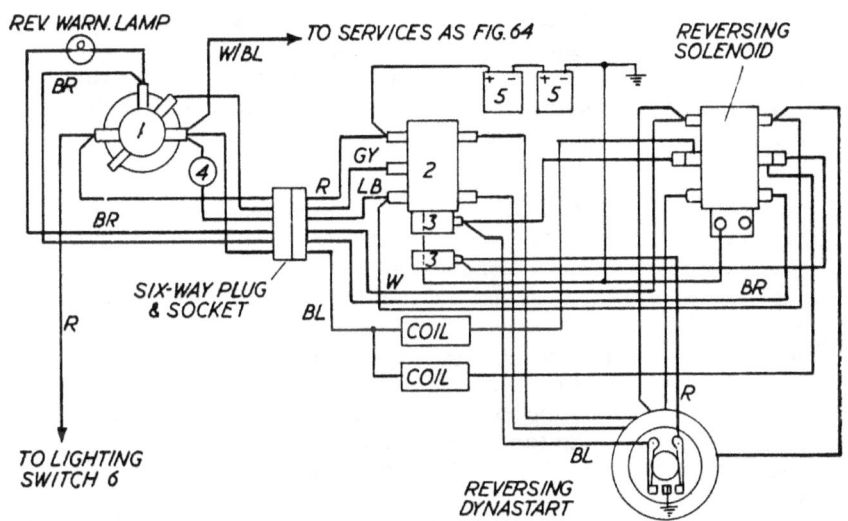

Fig. 65 (b). Wiring Diagram Mark "G" Twin with Reversible Dynastart

Main wiring to the ignition and starter switch only is shown. Wiring to the other services is as in Fig. 64.

left-hand set screw and screwing up the right-hand set screw tilts the beam to the *right*, and vice versa. For adjusting the horizontal height of the beam both set screws are either tightened or slackened equally, as required. Once having established a satisfactory alignment, tighten the lock nuts to ensure that the setting will not change due to vibration.

A point to watch in refitting a bulb is that the head and side contacts on the bulb are correctly made, and that the top position marked on the bulb stem is in the correct position when refitting the holder into the reflector.

The tail light is exposed simply by removing the two screws holding the lamp cover. Again check that the bulb is refitted the right way round so that maximum brilliance will operate on the "brake" side and not the normal tail light switching position. On later Mark "C" cars this original circuit will, however, inevitably have been reworked to incorporate twin tail lamps, which should be in accordance with the later Mark "C" wiring diagram shown in Fig. 60.

Here the stop light and number plate illuminating light are combined as a double-filament bulb (the higher-rated filament being the stop light) and separate twin tail lights of 6-watt rating are employed.

Mark "D." This model uses a 12-volt system and the headlights and sidelights are separate bulbs, although mounted in the same lamp housing. Access to the bulbs is by removing the two set screws on the lamp rim and withdrawing the glass and reflector from the lamp body. Adjustment of the headlamp beam is the same as for the Mark "C" models.

Mark "E" and Mark "F." The headlamps are built into the front wings and, to gain access to the bulbs, the rim must be removed by releasing the screw on the underside, the light unit pressed inwards against spring tension and then rotated in an anti-clockwise direction until it is free to be withdrawn. The bulb is then removed by twisting the cap in an anti-clockwise direction. Replacement follows the reverse order.

To adjust the headlamp beam, removal of the rim and rubber gasket seal discloses three spring-loaded screws. Vertical adjustment of the beam is provided by the top screw and sideways adjustment by the two side screws. Adjustment is logical, i.e. the beam is tipped in the direction of screwing-in.

Sidelights and front-flashing indicators are combined in double filament 6/21-watt bulbs. The bulb is reached by folding back the rubber sealing flange to allow the cover glass to be removed. The combined tail and stop-lights and the separate rear-winking-lights are reached by pushing the cover glasses in and twisting in an anti-clockwise direction until the glass and rim can be withdrawn. The number-plate lamp is reached by unscrewing its cover.

Mark "G." The headlamps are built into the front wings and adjustment is the same as for the Marks "E" and "F" via the three screws in the rim of the light unit revealed by removal of the rubber seal. Bulb replacement is likewise the same.

The side and front "winker" lamps are accessible by folding back the rubber sealing flange with the fingers to release the glass, when the bulbs can be removed from their bayonet fittings. In the case of the tail and stop lamps, or the rear "winker" lamps, push the lamp glass in and, by gripping on the four vanes, twist in an anti-clockwise direction until the glass with rim attached can be removed. The bulb is then readily accessible in its bayonet holder. The number plate lamp is reached by releasing the lamp cover retaining screw and removing the cover.

LAMP BULB SPECIFICATIONS

Mark "A." Headlamp: 6 V, 12/3 watt double filament.
Tail light: 6 V,* 3/3 watt double filament.

Mark "B." Headlamp: 6 V, 12/3 watt double filament.
Tail light: 6 V,* 3/3 watt double filament.

Mark "C." Early models—
Headlamp: 6 V, 12/3 watt double filament.
†Tail light: 6 V, 18/3 watt double filament.
With high-output generator—
Headlamp: 6 V, 18/3 watt double filament.
†Tail light: 6 V, 12/3 watt double filament.
Tail lights: 6 V, 6 watt.

Mark "D." Headlamp: 12 V, 24/24 watt double filament.
Side lamps: 12 V, 3 watt.
Tail and stop light: 12 V, 12/3 watt double filament.
Tail lights: 12 V, 6 watt.

Mark "E" and "F"
Headlamp: 12 V, 42/36 watt double filament (Mark "E" or "F")
12 V 24/24 watt double filament (Mark "F" only)
Side lamps: 12 V, 6/21 watt double filament. (combining flashers)
Tail and stop lights: 12 V, 6/21 watt double filament.
Rear flashers: 12 V, 21 watt.
Number plate lamp: 12 V, 4 watt.

* Applicable only to original model.
† Tail light on early models. Stop, number-plate light on later models.

Mark "G."   Headlamp: 12 V, 24/24 watt double filament with double contact base
Side and flasher lights: 12 V, 6/21 watt double filament, with double contact base
Twin tail and "stop" lights: 12 V, 6/21 watt double filament with double contact base
Rear flasher lights: 12 V, 21 watt single filament, single contact base
Number plate light: 12 V, 4 watt single filament single contact base
Panel light: 12 V, 2·2 watt miniature Edison screw type
Ignition warning light: 12 V, 1·2 watt special miniature bayonet cap
Neutral indicator light: 12 V, 2·2 watt miniature Edison screw type

"875" and "Ranger 875"
Headlamp: 50/40 watt pre-focus double filament with double contact base
Side lamps: 6 watt single filament with single contact base
Tail and stop lights: 6/21 watt double filament with double contact base
Front and rear flashers: 21 watt single filament with single contact base
Rear number plate light: 6 watt single filament with single contact base
Instrument panel light: 2·2 watt miniature Edison screw type
Headlamp main beam warning light: 2·2 watt miniature Edison screw type
Ignition warning light: 2·2 watt miniature Edison screw type
Flasher indicator warning light: 2·2 watt miniature Edison screw type
Oil pressure warning light: 2·2 watt miniature Edison screw type
 Note: all bulbs are 12 volt rating

CHAPTER XI

DYNASTART UNITS

DYNASTART electrical units are fitted to the Mark "D" De Luxe Minicar and all subsequent models. The uni-directional Dynastart unit provides electric starting and automatically-controlled battery charging. The reversible Dynastart unit provides, in addition, reverse direction of running for the engine (giving a reverse drive when a normal "forward" gear is engaged), by means of switching to a separate contact-breaker unit. Wiring diagrams appropriate to installation in Minicars are given in Figs. 62–65 in Chapter X.

An exploded view of the uni-directional Dynastart unit is given in Fig. 66 with component parts numbered and identified in the caption. This numbering is in accordance with the manufacturers' designation, although type numbers apply to each part which a Bond Minicar dealer can identify from a spare parts list.

The Dynastart unit consists, basically, of an armature, stator, contact breaker and cam, rather like a conventional magneto-generator except that the stator consists of twelve pole pieces, six of which carry starter windings, and six shunt windings. When driven by the engine the shunt windings are excited and generate current, both for lighting and ignition circuits. If, however, current is fed to the starter windings the unit operates as a series-wound motor, thus driving the engine for starting purposes.

The complete circuit also embraces an ignition coil and condenser, voltage regulator, cut out, ignition-starter switch and starter solenoid. The latter is controlled by a push button operating on an auxiliary circuit. The generated voltage is limited to a maximum of 12 volts by an automatic voltage control, remaining virtually constant and independent of engine speed. The cut-out switch closes at 12 volts to connect the battery for charging. Normal no-load voltage is approximately 15 volts but, as current is consumed, the voltage drops proportionately with output. The nominal charging rate is achieved at an engine speed of approximately 1,200 to 1,500 r.p.m. and, from this speed up, will accommodate a continuous load of up to 90 watts.

The contact-breaker unit is reached by removing the small cover plate on the starter housing and unscrewing the two screws which hold it in place (*see* Fig. 67). Little attention should be necessary other than a periodic checking and adjustment of the points gap. The gap is properly established by turning the engine until the piston is at top dead centre

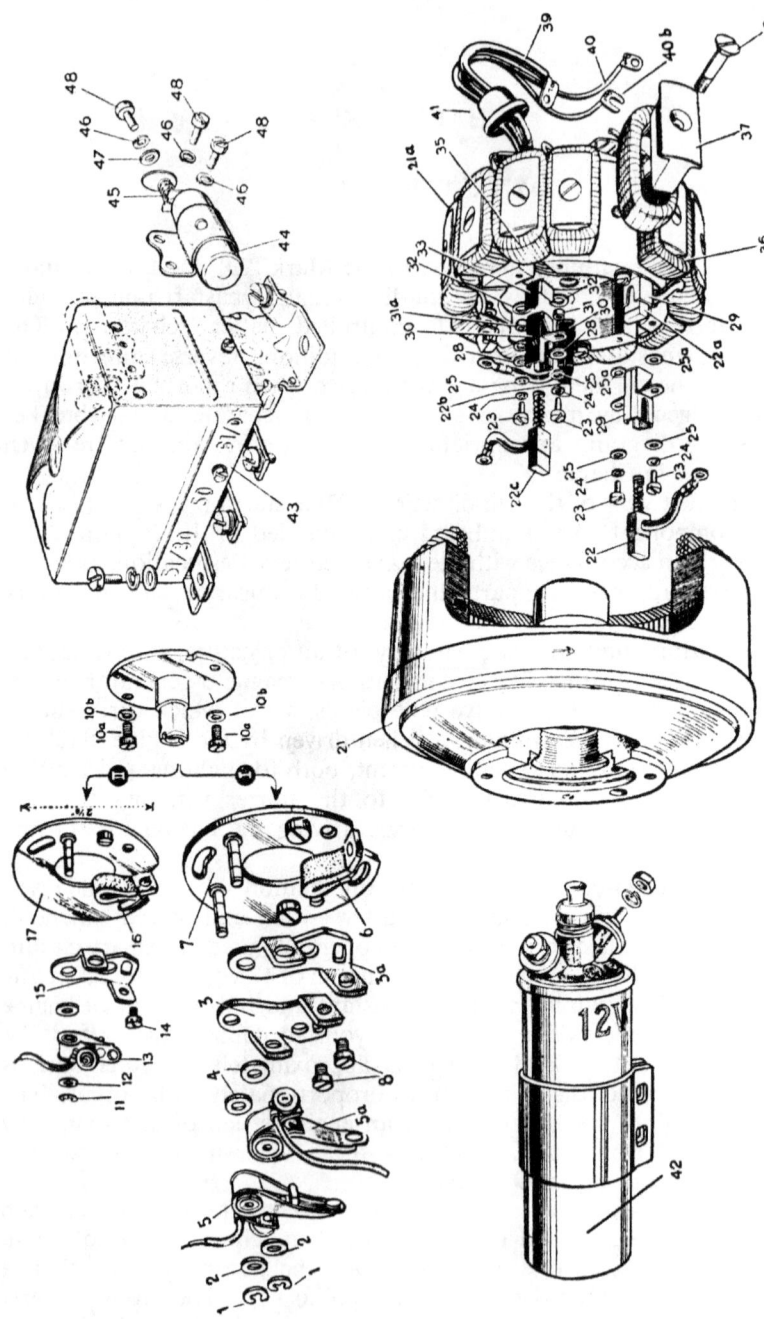

FIG. 66. EXPLODED VIEW OF THE SIBA DYNASTART UNI-DIRECTIONAL UNIT
(For key see page 105)

and then adjusting the gap to 0·020 in.–0·022 in. If the points are at all oily or dirty they should be cleaned by washing with petrol. It is seldom

FIG. 67. DYNASTART UNI-DIRECTIONAL INSTALLATION

The contact breaker is reached by removing the cover plate (arrowed).
1. Control box
2. Condenser
3. Ignition coil
4. Foot-starter retained for emergency starting (note pedal arm folds to one side)
5. High tension lead to plug.

good practice for the amateur mechanic to attempt to reface points if they have become pitted or burnt and, generally, in such circumstances a new set of points will be a more satisfactory answer.

KEY TO FIG. 66

Contact breaker (I)
3. Point bracket
3a. Point bracket
5. Rocker arm with cable
5a. Rocker arm with cable
6. Oiling pad
10. Fixed cam
Contact breaker (II)
13. Rocker arm with cable
15. Point bracket
17. Base plate with pin
22. Armature complete
21a. Stator

22. Carbon brush
22c. Carbon brush
29. Brush holder
33. Insulating sheath
35/36. Shunt and series winding
37/38. Poleshoe with screws
39. Starter cable
40. Generator cable
40b. HT cable
42. Ignition coil complete
43. Switch assembly box
44. Condenser
45. Cable clamp complete

(In this and similar illustrations only major items are listed.)

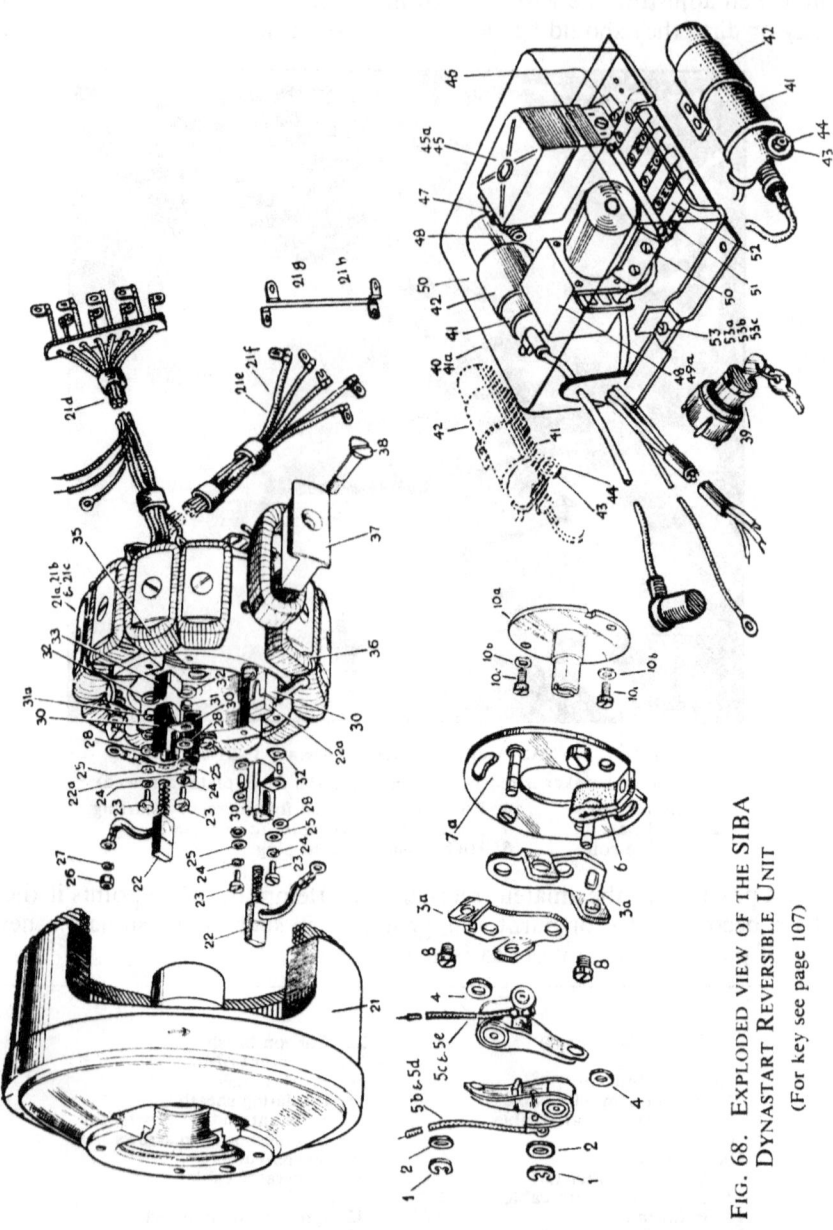

Fig. 68. Exploded view of the SIBA Dynastart Reversible Unit
(For key see page 107)

On some early models a points gap of 0·014 in.–0·016 in. was specified but it is generally agreed that the wider setting is to be preferred. If the engine was originally timed for the smaller opening, however, alteration of the setting will affect the timing and this will have to be readjusted (*see* Chapter VIII). Timing is altered by rotating the contact-breaker assembly *clockwise* to *retard* the ignition and *anti-clockwise* to *advance* it.

The manufacturers recommend that the armature be removed every 5,000 miles (or at six-monthly intervals, whichever is the shorter period), so that brushes can be examined for wear and particles of carbon dust, which may have accumulated, and cleaned out. Access to the armature is gained by removing the right-hand engine cover, the timing cam and the central hexagon nut. A special extractor is then screwed into the hub of the armature to withdraw it from the drive shaft.

To remove the stator, first disconnect the appropriate cables from the switch box and then remove the three socket-head screws holding the stator to the crankcase spigot and the four screws holding the inner housing to the crankcase. The stator and inner housing can then be lifted off.

When replacing, a gasket compound should be used on the mating faces of the stator and crankcase spigot. Check also that the crankcase oil seal is positioned correctly and the inner housing and cables properly lined up before replacing the stator and housing on the crankcase spigot. It is essential also that the lock washers be replaced under the socket-head screws and all screws tightened up in rotation to prevent possible distortion. Also carefully check the condition of the brushes and their freedom to move in the holders. The remainder of the assembly then follows the reverse order of dismantling, making sure that everything is correctly positioned and located. Rotate the armature by hand after tightening, to make sure that it is not fouling the stator.

The Dynastart reversible unit is basically similar (*see* Fig. 68), with the addition of a second contact-breaker unit for reverse timing controlled by a reversing solenoid. The ignition switch combines both the ignition switch and the starting and reversing solenoid contacts. On the Mark "D" two separate control or switch-assembly boxes are mounted on the engine unit (*see* Fig. 38), but all the controls and the ignition coil may be combined in a single control box.

KEY TO FIG. 68

3. Point bracket	33. Insulating sheath
5. Rocker arm	35. Shunt windings
7. Base plate	36. Series windings
10. Cam	37. Pole shoe
21*a, b, c.* Stator	39. Starter ignition switch
21*d, e, f.* Cable harness	40. Switch gear box
21*g, h.* Connecting cables	41. Ignition coil
22. Brush	45. Switch assembly box
30. Brush holder	48. Cable clamp
31. 31*a.* Fibre insert	49. Reversing solenoid

The contact-breaker is disclosed by removing the small cover plate on the right-hand cover as before, both contact-breaker rocker arms being mounted on a common base plate on separate pins. The fixed points are

Fig. 69. Reversible Dynastart Installation Showing the Cover Plate removed for access to the Contact-Breaker

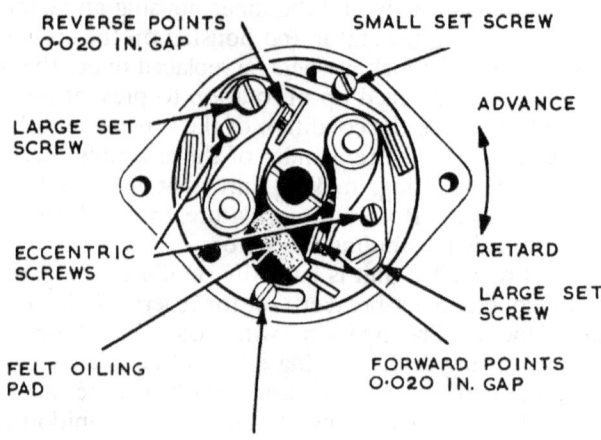

Fig. 69 (a). Contact-Breaker Unit of Mark "G"

carried on separate brackets, the best gap for the normal (forward running) points being 0·020 in.–0·022 in. As before, if the initial setting was of the order of 0·014 in., the timing will have to be adjusted to compensate for the increase in point movement.

Contact-breaker units on the 250 c.c. single- and twin-cylinder engines are shown in Figs 69 (a) and 69 (b), respectively. Gap adjustment, the same as on other models (0·020 in.), is adjusted by means of the cheese-headed eccentric screw after first slackening the large cheese-headed screw adjacent

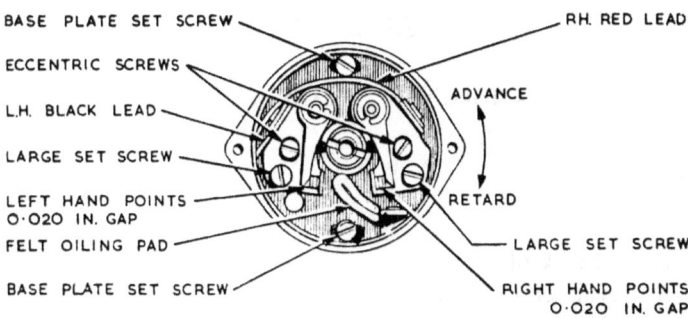

FIG. 69 (b). CONTACT-BREAKER UNIT OF MARK "G" TWIN

to it. On the reversing units the same procedure is followed on each contact-breaker.

Useful hints on routine maintenance and "trouble-shooting" with the Dynastart units will be found in Chapter IV dealing with fault finding.

APPENDIX I

ORIGINAL SPECIFICATIONS

MARK "A"

Engine

    Villiers, Mark 6E
    Single cylinder. 2-stroke
    Bore, 29 mm
    Stroke, 72 mm
    Cubic capacity: 197 c.c. = 11·71 cu. in.
    Engine sprocket: 19 teeth, $\frac{1}{2}$ in. pitch
    Sparking plug, Lodge HH14
    Sparking plug gap, 0·018 in.—0·025 in.
    Spark timing, $\frac{5}{32}$ in. before T.D.C.

Gearbox

    3 forward speeds
    Gearbox ratios—
        1st Gear 2·66 : 1
        2nd Gear 1·4 : 1
        3rd Gear 1 : 1
    Drive sprocket: 15 teeth $\frac{1}{2}$ in. pitch for Renold chain No. 110044
    Oil capacity, $\frac{3}{4}$ pint (approx.)

Carburettor

    Villiers type 4/5 two lever

Electrical System

    6-volt 10-amp/h battery

Fuel Capacity

    $2\frac{1}{2}$ gallons

Suspension

    Front coil spring and friction-type shock absorber (later, hydraulic shock absorber)

Tyres

    16·00 × 4·00 low pressure

Steering
Bobbin and cable (later rack and pinion)

Dimensions

	ft	in.
Wheel base	5	6
Track	4	2½
Overall length	8	9½
Overall width	4	10
Overall height	3	8
Ground clearance	—	5

Weight
340 lb

MARK "B"

Engine
Villiers, Mark 6E
Single cylinder. 2-stroke
Bore, 59 mm
Stroke, 72 mm
Cubic capacity: 197 c.c. = 11·71 cu. in.
Engine sprocket: 19 teeth, ½ in. pitch
Sparking plug, Lodge HH14
Sparking plug gap, 0·018 in.—0·025 in.
Spark timing, $\frac{5}{32}$ in. before T.D.C.

Gearbox
3 forward speeds
Gearbox ratios—
    1st Gear 2·66 : 1
    2nd Gear 1·4 : 1
    3rd Gear 1 : 1
Drive sprocket: 15 teeth ½ in. for Renold chain No. 110044
Oil capacity, ¾ pint (approx.)

Carburettor
Villiers type 4/5 two lever

Electrical System
6-volt 10-amp/h battery

Fuel Capacity
2½ gallons

Suspension
Front: coil spring and hydraulic shock absorber
Rear: coil spring (independent)

Tyres
4·00—8 low pressure

Dimensions

	ft	in.
Wheel base	5	6
Track	4	6
Overall length	9	1
Overall width	5	0
Overall height	3	9
Ground clearance	—	8

Weight
420 lb

MARK "C"

Engine
Villiers, Mark 8E
Single cylinder. 2-stroke
Bore, 59 mm
Stroke, 72 mm
Cubic capacity: 197 c.c. = 11·71 cu. in.
Engine sprocket: 23 teeth, $\frac{3}{8}$ in. pitch
Sparking plug, Lodge HH14
Sparking plug gap, 0·018 in.—0·025 in.
Spark timing, $\frac{5}{32}$ in. before T.D.C.

Gearbox
3 forward speeds
Gearbox ratios—
　　1st Gear 3·25 : 1
　　2nd Gear 1·7 : 1
　　3rd Gear 1 : 1
Drive sprocket: 19 teeth $\frac{1}{2}$ in. pitch for Renold chain No. 110044
Oil capacity, $\frac{3}{4}$ pint (approx.)

Carburettor
Villiers Type S.25

Electrical System
6-volt 10-amp/h battery (positive earth)

APPENDIX I

Fuel Capacity
    2½ gallons

Suspension
    Front: trailing arm and coil spring; hydraulic shock absorber
    Rear: bonded rubber units

Tyres
    4·00 × 8 low pressure

Steering
    Worm and sector

Dimensions

	ft	in.
Wheel base	5	6
Track	4	5
Overall length	9	10
Overall width	4	9
Overall height	4	2
Ground clearance	—	7

Weight
    460 lb

MARK "D"

Engine
    Villiers, Mark 9E/3
    Single cylinder. 2-stroke
    Bore, 59 mm
    Stroke, 72 mm
    Cubic capacity: 197 c.c. = 11·71 cu. in.
    Engine sprocket: 20 teeth, ⅜ in. pitch
    Sparking plug, Lodge HH14
    Sparking plug gap, 0·018 in.—0·025 in.
    Spark timing, $\frac{5}{32}$ in. before T.D.C.

Gearbox
    3 forward speeds
    Gearbox ratios—
        1st Gear 3·25 : 1
        2nd Gear 1·7 : 1
        3rd Gear 1 : 1
    Drive sprocket: 19 teeth ½ in. pitch for Renold chain No. 110046
    Oil capacity ¾ pint (approx.)

Carburettor

Villiers Type S.25

Electrical System

12 volt positive earth (two 6-volt 12-amp/h batteries)
12 volt Dynastart units on de-luxe models (negative earth)

Fuel Capacity

2½ gallons

Suspension

Front: trailing arm and coil spring hydraulic shock absorber
Rear: trailing arm and bonded rubber unit

Tyres

4·00 × 8 low pressure

Steering

Worm and sector

Dimensions

	ft	in.
Wheel base	5	6
Track	4	5
Overall length	9	10
Overall width	4	9
Overall height	4	2
Ground clearance	—	6½

Weight

520 lb

MARK "E"

Engine

Villiers, Mark 9E/4 SIBA or 9E/4 SIBA reversing
Single cylinder. 2-stroke
Bore, 59 mm
Stroke, 72 mm
Cubic capacity: 197 c.c. = 11·71 cu. in.
Engine sprocket: 20 teeth, ⅜ in. pitch
Sparking plug, Lodge HH14
Sparking plug gap, 0·018 in.—0·025 in.
Spark timing, $\frac{5}{32}$ in. before T.D.C.

Gearbox

4 forward speeds
Gearbox ratios—
   1st Gear 3·6 : 1
   2nd Gear 2·18 : 1
   3rd Gear 1·56 : 1
   4th Gear 1 : 1
Drive sprocket: 19 teeth ½ in. pitch for Renold chain No. 110046
Oil capacity, ¾ pint (approx.)

Carburettor

Villiers Type S.25

Electrical System

12 volt negative earth (two 6-volt 22·5-amp/h batteries)

Fuel capacity

3¼ gallons

Suspension

Front: trailing arm and coil spring; hydraulic shock absorber
Rear: trailing arm and bonded rubber unit

Tyres

4·00 × 8 low pressure

Steering

Worm and sector

Dimensions

	ft	in.
Wheel base	5	6
Track	4	5
Overall length	11	0
Overall width	5	0
Overall height	4	2
Ground clearance	—	6½

Weight

672 lb

MARK "F"

Engine

Villiers Mark 31A/4 SIBA or 31A/4 SIBA reversing
Single cylinder. 2-stroke
Bore, 66 mm
Stroke, 72 mm

Cubic capacity: 250 c.c. = 15·25 cu. in.
Engine sprocket: 20 teeth, ⅜ in. pitch
Sparking plug, Lodge HH14
Sparking plug gap, 0·018in.—0·025 in.
Spark timing, 5/32 in. before T.D.C.

Gearbox

4 forward speeds
Gearbox ratios—
    1st Gear 3·6 : 1
    2nd Gear 2·18 : 1
    3rd Gear 1·56 : 1
    4th Gear 1 : 1
Drive sprocket: 19 teeth ½ in. pitch for Renold Chain No. 110046
Oil capacity, ¾ pint (approx.)

Carburettor

Villiers Type S.25

Electrical system

12 volt negative earth (two 6-volt 22·5-amp/h batteries)

Fuel capacity

3¼ gallons

Suspension

Front: trailing arm and coil spring; hydraulic shock absorber
Rear: trailing arm and bonded rubber unit

Tyres

4·00 × 8 low pressure

Steering

Worm and sector

Dimensions

	ft	in.
Wheel base	5	6
Track	4	5
Overall length	11	0
Overall width	5	0
Overall height	4	2
Ground clearance	—	6½

Weight

672 lb

MARK "G"

Engine

    Villiers, Mark 35A/4 SIBA or 35A/4 SIBA reversing
    Single cylinder. 2-stroke
    Bore, 66 mm
    Stroke, 72 mm
    Cubic capacity: 250 c.c. = 15·25 cu. in.
    Engine sprocket: 20 teeth, $\frac{3}{8}$ in. pitch
    Sparking plug, Lodge HH 14
    Sparking plug gap, 0·018 in.—0·025 in.
    Spark timing, $\frac{5}{32}$ in. before T.D.C.

Clutch sprocket

    43 teeth $\frac{3}{8}$ in. pitch

Gearbox

    4 forward speeds
    Gearbox ratios—

        1st Gear 3·6 : 1
        2nd Gear 2·18 : 1
        3rd Gear 1·56 : 1
        4th Gear 1 : 1

    Drive sprocket: 22 teeth $\frac{1}{2}$ in. pitch for Renold chain No. 110046
    Oil capacity, $\frac{3}{4}$ pint (approx.)

Carburettor

    Villiers Type S25/8
        Main jet 150 c.c. (or 130 c.c. after 1,000 miles)
        Needle No. $3\frac{1}{2}$ (setting 1·95 in. from bottom of slide)

Ignition

    Coil

MARK "G" TWIN

Engine

    Villiers, Mark 4T/SK or 4T/SRK reversing
    Twin cylinder. 2-stroke
    Bore, 50 mm
    Stroke, 63·5 mm
    Cubic capacity: 250 c.c. = 15·25 cu. in.
    Engine sprocket: 25 teeth, $\frac{3}{8}$ in. pitch

Sparking plug, Lodge HH14
Sparking plug gap, 0·018 in.—0·025 in.
Spark timing, $\frac{5}{32}$ in. before T.D.C. (tolerance 0·155 in.–-0·175 in.)

Clutch sprocket

43 teeth, $\frac{3}{8}$ in. pitch

Gearbox

4 forward speeds
Gearbox ratios—
    1st Gear 4·0 : 1
    2nd Gear 2·22 : 1
    3rd Gear 1·55 : 1
    4th Gear 1 : 1
Drive sprocket: 17 teeth, $\frac{1}{2}$ in. pitch
Oil capacity, $\frac{3}{4}$ pint (approx.)

Carburettor

Villiers Type S25/11
  Main jet 250 c.c.
  Needle No $3\frac{1}{2}$ (setting 1·95 in. from bottom of slide)

Ignition

Twin coils

Electrical system

12 volt negative earth (two separate 6 volt, 25 amp/h capacity batteries)

Fuel system

$3\frac{1}{4}$ gallon fuel tank located at rear of bulkhead
Gravity feed from tank to carburettor
Fuel mixture: 16:1 petrol:SAE 30 oil

Suspension

Front: trailing arm controlled by coil spring with double-acting hydraulic shock absorber
Rear: trailing arm controlled by coil spring with double-acting hydraulic shock absorbers.

Tyres

4·00 × 10   front 36 lb/in.^{2} (all loads)
              rear 24–30 lb/in.^{2}

Steering

Worm and sector

Brakes

Lockheed hydraulic/mechanical (front brake operated hydraulically, rear brakes and handbrake mechanically)

Dimensions

	ft	in.
Wheelbase	5	6
Track	4	5
Overall length	11	0
Overall height	4	7
Ground clearance	—	7½

Weights

Single-cylinder engine (Car) 826 lb
Twin-cylinder engine (Car) 856 lb

BOND 875 AND BOND RANGER 875

Engine

Capacity: 875 c.c. (53·4 cu. in.)
Type: Overhead camshaft
Number of cylinders: 4
Nominal bore: 2·68 in. (68 mm)
Stroke: 2·38 in. (60·4 mm)
Distributor contact gap: 0·015 in. (0·38 mm)
Sparking plug type: Champion N9Y
Sparking plug gap: 0·025 in. (0·63 mm)
Compression ratio: 8·0:1
Oil pressure (hot) at 50 m.p.h. (80 k.p.h.) 50 lb. in.^{2} (3·5 kg. cm.^{2})

Ignition Timing—Static at full retard

3° (3 mm) B.T.D.C.
The mm dimension is measured on the periphery of the crankshaft pulley before the groove on the pulley reaches the pointer on the timing cover, on rotation of the engine.
Firing order: 1-3-4-2
No. 1 cylinder is next to the crankshaft pulley

Note The ignition setting given above may require slight variation according to the octane ratings of the fuels available.

Valve Timing

Inlet (intake) opens: 6° B.T.D.C.
Inlet (intake) Closes: 46° A.B.D.C.

Exhaust opens: 46° B.B.D.C.
Exhaust closes: 6° A.T.D.C.

Tappet Clearances
Inlet (intake): 0·004/0·006 in. (0·10/0·15 mm)
Exhaust: 0·010/0·012 in. (0·25/0·30 mm)

Carburettor Settings (Solex B.30 P.I.H.-5)
Choke (Venturi): 22 mm
Main jet: 115*
Pilot jet (slow running): 45
Pilot jet air bleed: 140
Econostat jet: 125
Air correction: 190

* 100 on export models with export type air cleaner.

Transaxle

Overall ratios (Synchromesh on all forward gears)
1st Gear 16·595:1
2nd Gear 8·905:1
3rd Gear 5·702:1
4th Gear 4·138:1
Reverse 13·824:1

Steering
Burman steering box: Worm and nut operation

Dimensions

Wheel base	6 ft 6 in. (198·12 cm)
Rear track	4 ft 0 in. (121·92 cm)
Overall length	10 ft 8 in. (325·12 cm)
Overall height	4 ft 3 in. (129·54 cm)
Overall width	4 ft 7 in. (139·7 cm)
Turning circle	28 ft 6 in. (868·68 cm)
Ground clearance	6 in. (15·24 cm)

Unladen Weight (approx): 881 lb (399·6 kg)

Tyre Maintenance

Size
135—12
(135—305)
Michelin X

APPENDIX I

Pressures

Front: 22 lb/in.^{2} (1·546 kg cm^2) All loads
Rear: 24 lb/in.^{2} (1·687 kg cm^2) Driver and passenger
Rear: 26 lb/in.^{2} (1·828 kg cm^2) Fully loaded

Capacities

Fuel capacity: 6 gal (7·2 U.S. gal; 27 litres)
Oil capacity—engine (with filter): $5\frac{1}{2}$ pt (6·6 U.S. pt; 3·1 litres)
Oil capacity—Transaxle: $4\frac{1}{2}$ pt (5·5 U.S. pt; 2·5 litres)
Oil capacity—steering box: $\frac{1}{8}$ pt (0·175 U.S. pt; 0·07 litres)
Coolant capacity (with heater): 11 pt (13·2 U.S. pt; 6·2 litres)
Battery capacity (12 V): 32 amp h
(*Negative earth*)

"875" and "RANGER 875" LUBRICANTS

Part	Lubricant	Recommended proprietary lubricants
Engine	SAE 20W	Castrolite; BP Visco-Static or Energol SAE 20W; Super-Shell Motor Oil or Shell X-100 20W; Esso Extra Motor Oil; Mobiloil Special.
Transaxle	SAE 80 EP	Castrol Hypoy Light; BP Gear Oil SAE 80 EP; Shell Spirax 80 EP; Esso Gear Oil GP 80; Mobilube GX 80.
Front wheel hub bearings	grease	Castrolease LM; BP Energrease L2; Shell Retinax A; Esso Multi-Purpose Grease H; Mobilgrease MP.
Rear wheel hub bearings	grease	Castrolease LM; BP Energrease L2; Shell Retinax A; Esso Multi-Purpose Grease H; Mobilgrease MP.
Steering box	SAE 90 EP	Castrol Hypoy; BP Gear Oil SAE 90 EP; Shell Spirax 90 EP; Esso Gear Oil GP 90/140; Mobilube GX 90.
Grease points*	grease	Castrolease LM; BP Energrease L2; Shell Retinax A; Esso Multi-Purpose Grease H; Mobilgrease MP.

* These comprise Steering Head Spindle, Leading Link Pivot, and Cam Profile.

Lubricant points which can be lubricated with ordinary engine oil (SAE 20) are: Shaft and cam bearing, contact-breaker pivot, automatic timing (spark) control, generator, hinges, locks and catches.

Hydraulic fluid (for brake and clutch master cylinders): Girling Brake Fluid SAE Spec 70 R.3.

APPENDIX II

MODIFICATIONS

Date	Modification	Remarks
November, 1951	Large sprocket fitted.	
December, 1951	New type rear spring and rubber buffers fitted.	from C/12/2428
January, 1952	New type braking system adopted.	from D/1/2507
February, 1952	"Easistart" decompressor fitted.	from D/2/2703
March, 1952	Michelin 4-ply tyres fitted as standard.	
May, 1952	Electric self-starter set made available as an accessory for fitment to existing cars.	
October, 1952	Straight-through steering column fitted.	
April, 1953	Straight-through silencer fitted.	from E/4/5594
April, 1953	Bonded rubber rear suspension (Mark "C" standard) made available as a conversion set for Mark "A" cars.	
July, 1953	Villiers 8E engine fitted. New method of chain adjustment. Grease nipple in reaction link. Choke cable reversed. Plug supressor fitted.	
September, 1953	"Covered-in" type of rear dust covers fitted to rear brake.	
September, 1953	Bush removed from reaction link.	
September, 1953	Engine stay fitted.	from E/7/5799
October, 1953	New windscreen fitted.	
November, 1953	New high-output generator fitted on Villiers 8E engine. Supply lead from coils taken to battery side of fuse.	from E/11/6112
January, 1954	Straight through steering and tubular trailing arm. "Armstrong" front spring and shock absorber fitted as standard.	
February, 1954	Bulkhead plate stiffened.	
March, 1954	Heavy-duty suspension adopted for "Minitrucks" and family models.	

APPENDIX II

Date	Modification	Remarks
May, 1954	Peg type sidescreens introduced.	
August, 1954	New type steering head bracket with additional top bolt.	
September, 1954	Twin rear lamps and reflectors fitted.	
October, 1954	Cross shaft brake pedal design adopted. Plastic lining, sloping seat, no cubby hole, pocket in lining. Knob on door handle, grab handle fitted. De luxe models fitted with front and rear bumpers.	
November, 1954	Burgess silencer fitted.	
November, 1954	Speedometer spindle fitted.	
November, 1954	S.25 carburettor fitted.	
November, 1954	Plastic (Fibreglass) rear wings adopted for de luxe and family models.	
October, 1955	Burgess cylindrical silencer fitted.	
January, 1956	Rear suspension unit modified.	
May, 1956	Mark "D" model introduced with Villiers 9E engine and SIBA electrical equipment.	
December, 1956	Mark "E" model introduced with stressed skin construction and four-speed gearbox.	
March, 1957	Ball race fitted in place of pressure washer.	
April, 1957	New front brake shoes and lining fitted.	
May, 1957	New Burgess silencer fitted (with two bolts).	
January, 1959	Mark "F" four-seater model introduced with 250 c.c. engine.	
August, 1962	Mark "G" introduced with 250 c.c. engine and car, van and estate bodies.	
March, 1963	Mark "G" Twin introduced with 250 c.c. twin-cylinder 2-stroke engine and same range of bodies.	
Late 1965	Prototype "875" appeared	
1967	Bond "875" and "Ranger8 75" introduced with Hillman Imp engine and Saloon or van versions.	

APPENDIX III

BOND MINICAR OWNERS' CLUB

THIS healthy and growing organization must surely be one of the most flexible of its kind in existence today, for its 30 or so separate groups are in fact completely separate, each making its own rules, arranging its own programmes and conducting its own domestic affairs quite independently of the others.

Nevertheless, these thirty Clubs are firmly bound in a common interest —the Bond Minicar—which is frequently and truthfully described as a "Bond of Friendship." It's a strange and heartening occurrence to notice Bond owners when they meet other Bond owners on the road. Without exception, such a meeting is marked by a flashing of lights, a cheery hand wave and a beaming smile, even when the Bond owners concerned are not Club members. And if a Bond should be stopped by the wayside, it's fairly certain that no other Bond will pass by until its owner has stopped and offered any assistance that may be necessary. Not that such help is often needed, but nevertheless, it is invariably offered.

The first Bond Minicar Owners' Club was started in Blackburn, Lancs. by a small group of enthusiasts in 1950. Their first Secretary, Mr. I. Marchant, was—and, at the time of writing, still is—Art Master at Blackburn Grammar School. Those pioneers were few in number but their enthusiasm was enormous, and in 1952 they staged their first Rally at Southport, an event which brought spectators and competitors from all over Britain. The Municipal Authorities at Southport allowed them half the coach park for the gathering.

When the Club organized a hill climb in the same year, they encountered all sorts of administrative difficulties. It was staged on a hill called Birdie Brow in the Ribble Valley, and the Club had no communications equipment such as is usual nowadays. For instance, to signal a "casualty" on the hill out of sight of the start and finish, a Club member stationed at the likeliest spot was armed with a Verey pistol! This in itself was no light undertaking, for it involved the securing of a Firearms Certificate and a special permit from the Air Ministry. And just to complicate matters still further, Birdie Brow is on both sides of the Lancs/Yorks border involving compliance with two sets of County Police requirements!

Since those early days however, Bond Minicar Owners' Club members have increased enormously in number and "know-how"; nowadays many of them stage sporting events which attract very big entries. None of these events, incidentally, can be classed as "speed events," in spite of the fact that often relatively high average speeds must be maintained. The interest, in fact, is much greater than the speed, as was evidenced by a recent Gymkhana held in Berkshire which attracted over a hundred entries. Two competitors curtailed their holiday in Devon, driving nearly two hundred miles specially to take part in the event, whilst another couple arrived back at their home in East Anglia from a Scottish Holiday and immediately drove on to the Berkshire rendezvous!

Today, there are Bond Minicar Clubs all over England, from Tees-side to Thames Valley, from the Lancashire coastline to East Anglia. Some of them have a membership of a dozen or so, whilst others can boast of over 100 members—all active members too. They receive neither direction of any kind from the makers of the Bond Minicar, nor financial assistance; but if help or guidance is required in any manner, it is freely given.

And when the Bond Minicar Club National Rally is held each year in Morecambe, that Lancashire resort can be sure of seeing in its streets on that week-end anything up to five or six hundred Bond Minicars. No wonder it is Britain's biggest "one-make" Rally!

One useful concession provided by Sharp's Commercials to Bond Minicar Owners' Club members, is automatic affiliation to the A.C.U., with the manufacturers paying the necessary affiliation fees. Clubs are, however, allowed to "contract-out" of this affiliation, if they so prefer.

So far as is known, the oldest member of a Bond Minicar Club—oldest in years that is, not in membership—is a gentleman from Reigate who at 71 years of age took part in the 1959 Morecambe Rally—his first competitive event. At the other end of the scale, a sixteen-year-old youngster from Manchester also took part, although the ink had barely dried on his provisional driving licence.

The distaff side is well represented too, for it is certain that any man who is married, betrothed, or otherwise entangled with the fairer sex loses no time in ensuring that the object of his attentions shares his enthusiasm for his Club and becomes an active member. Many of these devoted partners become as adept as their menfolk at diagnosing—and curing—troubles.

INDEX

ACCUMULATOR, 88, 93
Adjustment—
  brakes, 35-8
  carburettor, 54 *et seq.*
  chain, 39
  clutch, 33-5
  contact-breaker—
    6E, 52
    8E, 53
    9E, 64
  gearbox linkage, 39
  steering, 45-6
Armature, *see* Flywheel magneto

BATTERY, 88, 89, 90, 93
Body repairs, 49-51
Bond Minicar—
  Mark A, 1
  Mark B, 2
  Mark C, 3
  Mark D, 3, 5
  Mark E, 3, 4
  Mark F, 4, 5
  Mark G, 5
  "875", 6
  Ranger, 6
Brakes, 17, 35, 85
Bulb sizes, 101

CARBURETTOR, 15, 16, 54-8
  (S.25), 66
Chain, 40
Clutch, 33, 67
  adjustment, 33-5
Colour code, 87
Connecting rod, *see* Villiers engines
Constructional data, 4
Contact-breaker, 44, 52, 53, 64, 94 *et seq.*
Control layout—
  Mark A, 8
  Mark B, 8
  Mark C, 9
  Mark D, 10, 11, 12
  Mark E, 13, 14

Control layout—*(contd.)*
  Mark F, 13, 14
  Mark G, 15
Crankshaft, *see* Villiers engines
Cruising speeds, 2
Cylinder, *see* Villiers engines

DASHBOARD—
  Mark A, 8
  Mark B, 8
  Mark C, 9
  Mark D, 10, 12
  Mark E, 13, 14
  Mark F, 13, 14
  Mark G, 15
Dates of models, 1-6
Decarbonizing, 48-9
Decompressor, 43, 83
Dipstick, 18, 22
Driving 17
Dynastart, 95 *et seq.*, 103 *et seq.*

ELECTRICAL circuits—
  Mark A, 89
  Mark B, 89, 90
  Mark C, 90, 92, 94
  Mark D, 94, 95, 96
  Mark E, 97, 98
  Mark F, 97, 98
  Mark G, 97, 98
Electric starter, 3, 59 *et seq.*, 84
Emergency operation of lights, 88
Engine brace, 84

FACIA, *see* Dashboard
Fault finding, 29 *et seq.*
Fibreglass, 3, 4, 5
Flexitor unit, 2, 47, 80
Flywheel magneto—
  8E, 54
  9E, 65
Four-speed gearbox, 69
Front hub modification, 78
Front lamps, *see* Headlights
Fuel mixture, 15, 19, 20

INDEX

Fuel tap, 14, 15

GEARBOX—
  8E, 55
  9E (three-speed), 68
  9E (four-speed), 69
  Gearbox filler, 18
  Gearchange, 11
  Generator, see Villiers engines
  Generator, high output, 85
  Grease points, 23
  Grease specification, 26, 27

HARDTOP, 3
Headlight adjustment, 100, 101
Headlights, 98 et seq
High output generator, 85, 88, 91
Hillman Imp engine, 6
Hydraulic shock absorber, 78

IGNITION, 43
Ignition circuits, see Wiring diagrams
Ignition timing, 52, 65

JACK, 37
Jets, see Carburettor

LAMP bulb specifications, 101
Licence, 7
Lighting coil, see Flywheel magneto
Lights, 98
Linkage, brakes, 35, 85
Lubricants, tables, 26, 27, 121
Lubricating points, 22, 23
Lubrication table, 24, 25

MAGNETO—
  8E, 54
  9E, 65
Minitruck, 3
Minivan, 3
Models, see Bond Minicar

OIL points, 22, 23
Oil specification, 21
Oils, see Lubricants

PAINTWORK, 51
Perspex screen, 1
Petrol-oil mixture, 15, 26, 27
Plug gap, 29

Points gap, 30
Primary drive, 20
Production, 1–6

RANGER, 6
Rear hub, 78
Rear suspension, 2, 80
Rectifier, 87 et seq.
Registration, 7
Removing wheel, 37, 46
Reverse gear, 10, 11, 12, 14, see also Dynastart
Routine maintenance, 20 et seq.
Running-in, 19

SELF starter conversion, 59 et seq., 84
SIBA Dynastart, see Dynastart
Sidelights, 98–100
Silencer, 84
Slow running adjustment, 56
Spark plug, 44
Spark timing, 52, 65
Speedometer drive, 48
Speeds, 19
Spring link, 39
Starting technique, 16, 17
Stator, see Flywheel magneto
Steering—
  bobbin and cable, 45
  rack and pinion, 2, 45
  rack and pinion conversion, 76 et seq.
  worm and sector, 2, 45
Stub axle conversion, 78
Suspension—
  front, 78
  rear, 2, 45, 80

TAIL lamp, 98–100
Taxation, 7
Three-speed gearbox—
  8E, 60
  9E, 68
Timing adjustment—
  8E, 52
  9E, 65
Transmission, 39 et seq.
Triplex screen, 3
Tyre pressures, 25
Tyres, 46

VILLIERS engines—
  6E, 1, 52 et seq.
  8E, 3, 52 et seq.
  9E, 3, 63 et seq.
  Mark 31A, 250 c.c., 4, 5
  Mark 4T, 73, 74

WEEKLY maintenance, 24
Wheel removal, 37, 46
Wheel sizes, 6, Appendix 1

Windscreen wiper, 8 et seq.
Wiring colour code, 87
Wiring diagrams—
  Mark A, 89
  Mark B, 89, 90
  Mark C, 90, 92, 94
  Mark D, 94, 95, 96
  Mark E, 97, 98
  Mark F, 97
  Mark G, 97, 99

VELOCEPRESS MANUALS – MOTORCYCLE BY MAKE

AJS 1932-1948 SINGLES & TWINS 250cc THRU 1000cc (BOOK OF)
AJS 1945-1960 SINGLES 350cc & 500cc MODELS 16 & 18 (BOOK OF)
AJS 1955-1965 SINGLES 350cc & 500cc (BOOK OF)
ARIEL UP TO 1932 (BOOK OF)
ARIEL 1932-1939 PREWAR MODELS (BOOK OF)
ARIEL 1933-1951 (WORKSHOP MANUAL)
ARIEL 1939-1960 4 STROKE SINGLES (BOOK OF)
ARIEL 1958-1964 LEADER & ARROW (BOOK OF)
BMW R26 R27 (1956-1967) FACTORY WORKSHOP MANUAL
BMW R50 R50S R60 R69S (1955-1969) FACTORY WORKSHOP MANUAL
BRIDGESTONE 90 SERIES FACTORY WSM & PARTS CATALOGUE
BRIDGESTONE 175 SERIES FACTORY WSM & PARTS CATALOGUE
BRIDGESTONE 350 SERIES FACTORY WSM & PARTS CATALOGUES
BSA SERVICE SHEETS MASTER CATALOGUE ALL MODELS 1945-1967
BSA BANTAM D1 TO D7 1948-1966 FACTORY SERVICE SHEETS MANUAL
BSA BANTAM ALL MODELS FROM 1948 ONWARDS (BOOK OF)
BSA BANTAM D14 FACTORY WORKSHOP & INSTRUCTION MANUAL
BSA SINGLES & V-TWINS UP TO 1927 (BOOK OF)
BSA SINGLES & V-TWINS UP TO 1930 (BOOK OF)
BSA SINGLES & V-TWINS UP TO 1935 (BOOK OF)
BSA SINGLES & V-TWINS 1936-1939 (BOOK OF)
BSA C10, C11 & C12 1945-1958 FACTORY SERVICE SHEETS MANUAL
BSA OHV & SV SINGLES 250-600cc 1945-1959 (BOOK OF)
BSA C15 & B40 1958-1967 FACTORY SERVICE SHEETS MANUAL
BSA OHV & SV SINGLES 250cc (ONLY) 1954-1970 (BOOK OF)
BSA B31, B32, B33 & B34 1945-60 FACTORY SERVICE SHEETS MANUAL
BSA OHV SINGLES 350 & 500cc 1955-1967 (BOOK OF)
BSA M20, M21 & M33 1945-1963 FACTORY SERVICE SHEETS MANUAL
BSA TWINS A7 & A10 1948-1962 FACTORY SERVICE SHEETS MANUAL
BSA TWINS A7 & A10 1948-1962 (BOOK OF)
BSA TWINS A50 & A65 1962-1965 FACTORY WORKSHOP MANUAL
BSA TWINS A50 & A65 1962-1969 (SECOND BOOK OF)
DOUGLAS 1929-1939 PREWAR ALL MODELS (BOOK OF)
DOUGLAS 1948-1957 POSTWAR ALL MODELS FACTORY SHOP MANUAL
DUCATI 160cc, 250cc & 350cc OHC MODELS FACTORY SHOP MANUAL
HONDA 50 ALL MODELS UP TO 1970 INC MONKEY & TRAIL (BOOK OF)
HONDA 90 ALL MODELS UP TO 1966 (BOOK OF)
HONDA 125-150cc TWINS C/CS/CB/CA FACTORY WORKSHOP MANUAL
HONDA 250-305 TWINS C/CS/CB FACTORY WORKSHOP MANUAL
HONDA 450 CB/CL 1965-1974 K0 TO K7 WORKSHOP MANUAL
HONDA C100 SUPER CUB FACTORY WORKSHOP MANUAL
HONDA C110 SPORT CUB 1962-1969 FACTORY WORKSHOP MANUAL
HONDA TWINS & SINGLES 50cc THRU 305cc 1960-1966 (BOOK OF)
HONDA TWINS ALL MODELS 125cc THRU 450cc UP TO 1968 (BOOK OF)
INDIAN PONYBIKE, BOY RACER & PAPOOSE ILL PARTS LIST & SALES LIT
J.A.P. ENGINES 1927-1952 & MOTORCYCLES 1934-1952 (BOOK OF)
MATCHLESS 1931-1939 ALL MODELS 250cc THRU 990cc (BOOK OF)
MATCHLESS 1945-1956 350 & 500cc SINGLES (BOOK OF)
MATCHLESS 1955-1966 350 & 500cc SINGLES (BOOK OF)
NEW IMPERIAL ALL SV & OHV FROM 1935 ONWARDS (BOOK OF)
NORTON 1932-1939 PREWAR MODELS (BOOK OF)
NORTON 1932-1947 (BOOK OF)
NORTON 1938-1956 (BOOK OF)
NORTON 1955-1963 MODELS 19, 50 & ES2 (BOOK OF)
NORTON 1955-1965 DOMINATOR TWINS (BOOK OF)
NORTON 1960-1970 TWIN CYLINDER FACTORY WORKSHOP MANUAL
NORTON 1970-1975 COMMANDO FACTORY WORKSHOP MANUAL
NORTON 1975-1978 MK 3 COMMANDO FACTORY WORKSHOP MANUAL
NSU QUICKLY 1953-1963 ALL MODELS (BOOK OF)
PANTHER 1932-1958 LIGHTWEIGHT MODELS 250 & 350cc (BOOK OF)
PANTHER 1938-1966 HEAVYWEIGHT MODELS 600 & 650cc (BOOK OF)
RALEIGH MOPEDS 1960-1969 (BOOK OF)
RALEIGH MOTORCYCLES 1919-1933 (BOOK OF)
ROYAL ENFIELD 1934-1946 SINGLES & V TWINS (BOOK OF)
ROYAL ENFIELD 1937-1953 SINGLES & V TWINS (BOOK OF)
ROYAL ENFIELD 1946-1962 SINGLES (BOOK OF)
ROYAL ENFIELD 1958-1966 250cc & 350cc SINGLES (SECOND BOOK OF)
ROYAL ENFIELD 736cc INTERCEPTOR FACTORY WORKSHOP MANUAL
RUDGE 1933-1939 (BOOK OF)
SUNBEAM 1928-1939 (BOOK OF)
SUNBEAM 1946-1957 S7 & S8 (BOOK OF)
SUZUKI 50cc & 80cc UP TO 1966 (BOOK OF)
SUZUKI T10 1963-1967 FACTORY WORKSHOP MANUAL
SUZUKI T20 & T200 1965-1969 FACTORY WORKSHOP MANUAL
SUZUKI TWINS 1962 ONWARDS 125-500cc WORKSHOP MANUAL
TRIUMPH 1935-1939 PREWAR MODELS (BOOK OF)
TRIUMPH 1935-1949 (BOOK OF)
TRIUMPH 1937-1951 (WORKSHOP MANUAL)
TRIUMPH 1945-1955 FACTORY WORKSHOP MANUAL
TRIUMPH 1945-1958 TWINS (BOOK OF)
TRIUMPH 1956-1969 TWINS (BOOK OF)
VELOCETTE 1925-1970 ALL SINGLES & TWINS (BOOK OF)
VILLIERS ENGINE UP TO 1959 INC. 3 WHEELERS (BOOK OF)
VILLIERS ENGINE UP TO 1969 (BOOK OF)
VINCENT 1935-1955 (WORKSHOP MANUAL)
YAMAHA 1961-1967 YA5 & YA6 (WORKSHOP MANUAL & ILL PARTS LIST)
YAMAHA 1971-1972 JT1 & JT2 (WORKSHOP MANUAL & ILL PARTS LIST)

VELOCEPRESS TECHNICAL BOOKS – MOTORCYCLE

1930'S BRITISH MOTORCYCLE CARBS & ELEC COMPONENTS (BOOK OF)
1930'S BRITISH MOTORCYCLE ENGINES (OVERHAUL & MAINTENANCE)
1930'S BRITISH MOTORCYCLE GEARBOXES & CLUTCHES (BOOK OF)
CATALOG OF BRITISH MOTORCYCLES (1951 MODELS)
CYCLEMOTOR (BOOK OF)
LUCAS ELECTRONICS BRITISH M/CYCLES REPAIR & PARTS (1950-1977)
MOTORCYCLE ENGINEERING (P.E. Irving)
MOTORCYCLE ROAD TESTS 1949-1953 (Motor Cycle Magazine UK)
SPEED AND HOW TO OBTAIN IT (Motor Cycle Magazine UK)
TUNING FOR SPEED (P.E. Irving)

VELOCEPRESS MANUALS – SCOOTERS BY MAKE

BSA SUNBEAM SCOOTER WORKSHOP MANUAL 1959-1965
BSA SUNBEAM SCOOTER 1959-1965 (BOOK OF)
LAMBRETTA 1947-1957 ALL 125 & 150cc MODELS (BOOK OF)
LAMBRETTA 1957-1970 LI & TV MODELS (SECOND BOOK OF)
NSU PRIMA 1956-1964 ALL MODELS (BOOK OF)
TRIUMPH TIGRESS SCOOTER WORKSHOP MANUAL 1959-1965
TRIUMPH TIGRESS SCOOTER (BOOK OF)
VESPA 1951-1961 (BOOK OF)
VESPA 1955-1963 125 & 150cc & GS MODELS (SECOND BOOK OF)
VESPA 1955-1968 GS & SS (BOOK OF)
VESPA 1963-1972 90, 125 & 150cc (THIRD BOOK OF)

VELOCEPRESS MANUALS - THREE WHEELER'S

BOND MINICAR THREE WHEELER (BOOK OF)
BMW ISETTA FACTORY WORKSHOP MANUAL
BSA THREE WHEELER (BOOK OF)
VINTAGE MORGAN THREE WHEELER (BOOK OF)

VELOCEPRESS MANUALS – AUTOMOBILE BY MAKE

ALFA ROMEO GIULIA WORKSHOP MANUAL 1300 TO 2000cc 1962-1975
ALFA ROMEO GIULIA TECH MANUAL CARBURETED CARS FROM 1962
ALFA ROMEO GIULIA TECH MANUAL FUEL INJECTED CARS FROM 1969
ALFA ROMEO GIULIETTA & GIULIA 750 & 101 SERIES 1955-1965 WSM
AUSTIN-HEALEY SPRITE & MG MIDGET WORKSHOP MANUAL 1958-1971
BMW 600 LIMOUSINE FACTORY WORKSHOP MANUAL
BMW 600 LIMOUSINE OWNERS HAND BOOK & SERVICE MANUAL
BMW 2000 & 2002 1966-1976 WORKSHOP MANUAL
CORVAIR 1960-1969 WORKSHOP MANUAL
CORVETTE V8 1955-1962 WORKSHOP MANUAL
FIAT 500 FACTORY WORKSHOP MANUAL 1957-1973
FIAT 600, 600D & MULTIPLA FACTORY WORKSHOP MANUAL 1955-1969
JAGUAR E-TYPE 3.8 & 4.2 SERIES 1 & 2 WORKSHOP MANUAL
JAGUAR MK 7, 8, 9 & XK120, 140, 150 WORKSHOP MANUAL 1948-1961
METROPOLITAN FACTORY WORKSHOP MANUAL
MGA & MGB OWNERS HANDBOOK & WORKSHOP MANUAL
MG MIDGET TC, TD, TF & TF1500 WORKSHOP MANUAL
PORSCHE 356 1948-1965 WORKSHOP MANUAL
PORSCHE 911 2.0, 2.2, 2.4 LITRE 1964-1973 WORKSHOP MANUAL
PORSCHE 911 2.7, 3.0, 3.2 LITRE 1973-1989 WORKSHOP MANUAL
PORSCHE 912 WORKSHOP MANUAL
TRIUMPH TR2, TR3, TR4 1953-1965 WORKSHOP MANUAL
VOLKSWAGEN TRANSPORTER, TRUCKS & WAGONS 1950-1979 WSM
VOLVO 1944-1968 ALL MODELS WORKSHOP MANUAL

VELOCEPRESS TECHNICAL BOOKS - AUTOMOBILE

FERRARI 250/GT SERVICE AND MAINTENANCE
FERRARI GUIDE TO PERFORMANCE
FERRARI OWNER'S HANDBOOK
FERRARI TUNING TIPS & MAINTENANCE TECHNIQUES
HOW TO BUILD A FIBERGLASS CAR
HOW TO BUILD A RACING CAR
HOW TO RESTORE THE MODEL 'A' FORD
MASERATI OWNER'S HANDBOOK
OBERT'S FIAT GUIDE
PERFORMANCE TUNING THE SUNBEAM TIGER
SOUPING THE VOLKSWAGEN
SOLEX CARBURETORS (EMPHASIS ON UK & EU AUTOMOBILES)
SU CARBURETORS (EMPHASIS ON UK AUTOMOBILES)
WEBER CARBURETORS (EMPHASIS ON ALFA & FIAT)

VELOCEPRESS BOOKS & GUIDES - AUTOMOBILE

ABARTH BUYERS GUIDE
COMPLETE CATALOG OF JAPANESE MOTOR VEHICLES
FERRARI 308 SERIES BUYER'S AND OWNER'S GUIDE
FERRARI BERLINETTA LUSSO
FERRARI BROCHURES AND SALES LITERATURE 1946-1967
FERRARI BROCHURES AND SALES LITERATURE 1968-1989
FERRARI SERIAL NUMBERS PART I - ODD NUMBERS TO 21399
FERRARI SERIAL NUMBERS PART II - EVEN NUMBERS TO 1050
FERRARI SPYDER CALIFORNIA
HENRY'S FABULOUS MODEL "A" FORD
MASERATI BROCHURES AND SALES LITERATURE

VELOCEPRESS BOOKS – RACING

CARRERA PANAMERICANA - MEXICAN ROAD RACE (BOOK OF)
DIALED IN - THE JAN OPPERMAN STORY
IF HEMINGWAY HAD WRITTEN A RACING NOVEL
VEDA ORR'S NEW REVISED HOT ROD PICTORIAL

AUTOBOOKS WORKSHOP MANUALS & BROOKLANDS ROAD TEST PORTFOLIOS

FOR A COMPLETE LISTING OF THE AUTOBOOKS & BROOKLANDS TITLES THAT WE CURRENTLY HAVE AVAILABLE, PLEASE VISIT OUR WEBSITE.
www.VelocePress.com

Please visit our website

www.VelocePress.com

for a complete up-to-date list of titles, descriptions, and secure online ordering using PayPal.

www.ingramcontent.com/pod-product-compliance
Lightning Source LLC
Chambersburg PA
CBHW070554170426
43201CB00012B/1840